TO MOSS!!
DIG IN!!...
ALL CHEERS

FOR:

ENJOY
THE BOOK
AND THE
FOOD IS
PRODUCT X

BEN.

tapas

tapas

simple combinations   striking flavours

El Parador

carlos horrillo & patrick morcas

photography by gus filgate

kyle books

This paperback edition first published in Great Britain in 2010 by Kyle Books
an imprint of Kyle Cathie Ltd.
67–69 Whitfield Street, London, W1T 4HF
general.enquiries@kylebooks.com
www.kylebooks.com

First published in hardback in 2008 by Kyle Cathie Ltd.

ISBN: 978 1 85626 950 6

A CIP catalogue record for this title is available from the British Library

10 9 8 7 6 5 4 3

Carlos Horrillo and Patrick Morcas are hereby identified as the author of this work in accordance with section 77 of Copyright, Designs and Patents Act 1988.

Text copyright © 2008 by Carlos Horrillo and Patrcik Morcas
Photographs copyright © 2008 by Gus Filgate
Design copyright © 2008 by Kyle Books

Project editor: Sophie Allen
Copy editor: Catherine Ward
Proofreader: Stephanie Evans
Design: Lizzie Ballantyne
Photography: Gus Filgate
Props: Penny Markham
Production: Sha Huxtable

contents

introduction

Patrick and I have been best friends since school. After school and university we both had various jobs in catering, helping each other out in our respective restaurants whenever needed. Then one day, God knows how it cropped up, we decided to open up a restaurant. Spanish tapas seemed to be the theme of the day; my father and mother were always cooking lovely traditional dishes at home and Patrick and I loved that way of eating… basically, it seemed a good idea at the time.

We could not afford a lot, so our original idea of opening up a nice long bar that people could sit and eat at as well as having a 60/70 seater restaurant where people could chill out… was pared down to a small 30/40 seater restaurant with an extra room downstairs (the garden terrace came after the first couple of years), in the unknown area of Mornington Crescent. We were originally going to call it 'Tapa, pan y vino'…'Tapa, bread and wine', but we thought it to be a bit of a mouthful. (It makes us chuckle that Fergus Henderson, Chef/Proprietor of St Johns, opened up a place called Bread and Wine.) So, after a reconnaissance mission to Madrid before we opened, we decided to call our restaurant El Parador.

We wanted to create an unfussy, simple place. It had to be easy to operate, and a place in which our punters would feel at ease. Our lack of finance dictated the simplicity and, as front of house, we created the rest. Since before we opened, family ties have always been there to help us along. Patrick's aunt loaned us some money to start up with. My father-in-law financed our weekend trip to Madrid. My parents helped us with the recipes. My wife, Sarah, and a close friend of ours, Candace Bahouth, did the mosaic on the bar fascia. Juliet, Patrick's sister, and Rowan, his nephew, have been helping us to run the show almost since day one. Patrick's brother-in-law, Cob, now helps Hamdi, our Head Chef run the kitchen. Hamdi has been with us nearly ten years.

Simple food: unfussy, uncomplicated and easy to cook. Both Patrick and I can cook every dish on the menu. It is cooking for large numbers of people, and consistently doing it well, where Hamdi and Cob leave us in their wake. Our first menu was by and large full of classic dishes that my parents gave us. Chris and Gary were our chefs: two guys who could cook and liked Spain a lot; those were their credentials. The four of us would sit down and work out ideas and dishes that could best be produced from our small kitchen. This is what we still do today, except today there are five of us as Juliet has her input. We change our menu twice a year. It takes two to three months for people to be prised away from their favourite dishes and introduced to the new ones that in turn become their favourites as well. So we thought it best not to change the menu too often. We put ideas on the table, discuss them and work them through. If we come across a dish that we like but is too complicated to produce, that is, there are too many movements for one chef (the chefs often operate on their own), we break it down, and rebuild it with the main ingredient first, then carry on adding what we think is

Above: Carlos's family in the delicatessen that they owned in Malaga, Spain.

essential, then stop when the dish feels like it has enough strength of flavour and can stand on its own. So, lots of time is spent staring into space... imagining flavours... and colours... the dish has also got to be aesthetically pleasing. Although our menu is predominantly Spanish in flavour and style (insofar it is served in 'tapa' form), it does contain dishes that are more Mediterranean than just Spanish. As you all know by now, proper tapas are small servings. We serve something more substantial. It is usually called a 'racion' in Spain, literally translated, this means 'portion', and that is exactly what we serve at El Parador, good, healthy-sized portions.

Patrick and I eat out a lot... hey, I know, someone's got to do it. We often bring ideas to our meetings that we have seen elsewhere and then reconstruct them to make them our own. After confirming it with the 'board', it goes on the menu. The hard work comes with the 'mise en place' (the preparation). The roasting of the chilli tomatoes; the roasting of the garlic; the charring and peeling of the red peppers; the preparation in advance of certain dishes like the octopus and the stews. All this needs prepping before service; all this needs organisation by Hamdi and Cob so that during the final cooking stage everything goes without a hitch.

So, how is it all done? These recipes are based on servings of 4, 6 or 8. At El Parador we serve all our dishes separately – if you order four portions of tuna, you will get four separate portions. You can do just that when you serve them at home or put them all on one big plate for everyone to dig in. Customers usually order 2 to 3 dishes per person and then share them, mixing and matching their choices to create their meal. So when you're cooking, select a couple of dishes that you think would go well together, and create your own 'feast'.

cooking notes

preparing things in advance

As you read through the recipes, you will begin to appreciate the preparatory work our chefs Hamdi, Cob, Jack and August have to carry out. In a restaurant, the preparation happens long before service. And the same principle should apply at home. When you choose a recipe, have a quick read through and check out what can be done in advance. Some recipes are really simple to cook, but the ingredients might need marinating for several hours beforehand. Other dishes might include items, such as roasted cherry tomatoes or chargrilled peppers, that can be prepped several hours before you cook the rest of the dish. The chicken stews can be made a whole day in advance and stored in the fridge (which actually improves their flavour). There are many other examples of how you can save yourself time – cooking for yourself and friends should be fun, not a burden.

browning and caramelising

Browning requires patience and vigilance as you watch and slowly turn the raw ingredients into something a golden brown colour.

If you are browning garlic, onions or other vegetables (also called 'sweating'), this is done over a very low heat and takes up to 15–20 minutes for the vegetables to turn soft and golden. During this time it is advisable to give the pan a few gentle shakes.

When you want to sauté vegetables so they are 'browned' on the outside yet firm on the inside, then this is done over a high heat, with smoking hot oil. The vegetables need to be stirred regularly to avoid burning them. When they start to brown, taste them, and remove when they are to your liking.

With meat and fish the process requires the pan or griddle to be smoking hot so you are cooking over a high heat. When you place the ingredient on the hot pan/griddle, the flesh will instantly brown within 20–30 seconds – this is called 'searing'. This seals any moisture inside the body of the flesh, allowing it to remain tender and juicy throughout the remaining cooking period. If you try and lift the ingredients too early, it will stick and tear; leave it too long and it will cook through too much, and any subsequent cooking will dry the flesh out. So when you place the ingredient on the pan/griddle, let it sear for 20–30 seconds, then with a palette knife, lift it up to see if the flesh is browned, then ease it over onto the other side and let it sear for another 20–30 seconds. Remove from the heat and carry on with the rest of the cooking.

If you place too many pieces of fish or meat on the pan/griddle at the same time, there is a chance that the heat will dissipate, and will boil the meat/fish (if there is a little liquid) instead of searing it. That is why we suggest cooking certain recipes in batches, keeping the first batch warm in a low oven whilst you cook the remaining ingredients before marrying them together for the final seconds of cooking.

frying pans and other equipment

I recommend using heavy-based pans because they will retain and transfer heat better. Try and use the largest pan you have available to avoid cramming the food in the pan. This will prevent the contents cooking unevenly. If you have a medium-sized pan it is far better to cook the ingredients in two separate batches rather than trying to cook everything at once.

A large, cast-iron griddle plate is a great piece of equipment for 'grilling' food without adding lots of oil. If you haven't got one already, I really recommend you invest in one and, once again, it's worth investing in the largest one you can afford. The best sort has a flat surface on one side and ridges on the other, and is designed to fit across two rings on the stove. The ridged side will leave the meat or fish with score marks, the flat side is ideal for grilling food that does not require a lot of oil. Before using it for the first time, make sure you 'season' your griddle (as you would a wok) by rubbing it with an oily rag (or kitchen paper), and then placing it on a high heat until it starts to smoke. You should then let it cool, and then turn it over and repeat on the other side.

sea salt

Throughout the book I will be recommending you use Maldon sea salt. If salt can have any flavour, this sea salt has it. Its crystals do not have the bitter aftertaste that most salts have and because it is pure and quite intense, you do not have to use so much when you cook. Before you season your food at any time, always taste it. This is very important if you are cooking ingredients with some salt content, such as salt cod and samphire, and if you are using salted butter.

When it comes to marinating meat or fish, it is advisable not to add salt because, like lemon juice, salt 'cooks' the meat/fish, if left on them for long periods. The salt should be added later when you start to cook.

basic stocks

The advantage of roasting a chicken whole is that you get to boil up the bones afterwards to make chicken stock – always handy for stews, casseroles and paellas to give them extra flavour. Once you have picked as much meat off the chicken as possible (for sandwiches or whatever), put the carcass into a large saucepan and cover it with cold water. Add a roughly chopped carrot, celery stick and medium leek, plus a bay leaf and a couple of pinches of salt and pepper. Bring to the boil, and then simmer for 2 hours (topping up with water, if necessary). Strain through a sieve and store in the fridge or freezer until needed.

For vegetable stock, place 1.5 litres of water in a large saucepan with a roughly chopped stick of celery, large carrot and large onion or leek. Add a couple of bay leaves, a few black peppercorns and some salt, and then bring to the boil. Turn down the heat and simmer for 90 minutes. Strain through a nylon sieve and store in the fridge or freezer until needed.

olive oil

When you read through the recipes, you'll see that I use 'dashes' to describe how much olive oil to use. Most olive oil bottles come with some sort of plastic top to help pouring. If you are using your own bottle then you will need to buy a pourer, like the ones used in bars (you can buy them at any good kitchenware shop). Once the pourer is in, grab the bottle by the neck and turn it to pour. It will pour steadily. While the bottle is in this position, give it a quick jerk down and the oil will dash out, instead of pour. After a couple of attempts you will get the hang of it. Always try to use good-quality olive oil. There are plenty to choose from that suit all palates. As a rule of thumb, at El Parador, we usually use normal olive for frying, virgin and extra virgin olive oil for certain marinades and occasional frying which requires rich, olive oil overtones, and then the light olive oil for salad dressings.

infused olive oils and garlic confit

Infused olive oils are a brilliant way of adding instant flavour to grilled meats, fish or vegetables. The most common ones are garlic- or chilli-infused oils, although you can use any kind of herbs as well. To make them at home, take a 750ml wine bottle, clear preferably – if you have an 'interesting' looking bottle so much the better – and fill it almost to the top with good, ordinary olive oil. Stuff in 4 large garlic cloves or chillies (or a combination of both). The oil will coat the ingredients you are infusing. Once the oil level drops and exposes them, they will start to deteriorate within a couple of days so it is best to clean out the bottle thoroughly and start again. Don't be tempted to top up the oil. If you do not use your infused oil very often, store it away from sunlight and use within 4–6 weeks.

Our chefs also keep to hand a container with whole garlic cloves that have been gently fried in olive oil. They are steeped in their own juices, which leaves them almost sweet and nutty, yet not too intense. This describes the cooking term 'confit'. The chefs often add the garlic cloves or the oil to many dishes as they are being cooked.

harissa

This is a North African chilli paste found mainly in Algeria and Tunisia, made with caraway, coriander and cumin seeds, garlic and red or green (hot) chillies in large quantities, lemon juice and if so desired, a pinch of smoked paprika. You can make it yourself but there are now very good tinned brands in supermarkets and delicatessens. Some of them can lack a bit of substance, but you can compensate by adding more of any of the prime ingredients yourself and whizzing them all up again; just remember to keep a balance of the flavours. Harissa will keep for several days in the fridge if you float some olive oil on its surface.

dips

We first introduced dips to El Parador in our second year. We thought that maybe our customers would like something to munch on while they waited for the other tapas. Alioli was, of course, a definite; and then one came from a friend, and the other from good old mum.

Alioli

We make our alioli with sunflower oil, but you can use a mixture of half sunflower and half olive oil, if you wish. Just bear in mind that too much olive oil will make the alioli very, very rich and also very thick, so you'll end up having to dilute it. You can dollop alioli on anything – from vegetables and potatoes to fish or meat, or even hunks of bread. It will keep for up to 2–3 days in an airtight container in the fridge.

Makes
1 litre

3 **egg yolks**
4 **garlic cloves,** peeled and crushed
Maldon sea salt, to taste
1 litre **sunflower oil** (or half sunflower and half olive oil)

Combine the eggs, garlic and a pinch of salt in a food-processor, and set it off at a slow speed. Start to drizzle in the olive oil in a slow, steady stream and keep on blitzing until the mixture begins to thicken. Carry on adding the oil, keeping the machine running, until you have a rich, creamy mayonnaise. If the mixture is too runny, or it separates, add another egg yolk and keep blending. If it is too thick, add a few tablespoons of cold water to thin it. Season to taste with salt (you can add pepper if you wish). Once it is made, you can add other ingredients to alter the alioli's flavour, including chillies, saffron, fresh rosemary or tarragon, wholegrain mustard or harissa. Just bear in mind that if you add something that could possibly thicken it – such as mustard or harissa – you will need to thin it again afterwards with water.

Puré de Habas Verdes

Puréed broad beans with pan-fried garlic, rosemary and olive oil

My mother used to make a great lentil stew. The thing I was never so keen on was her version of puréed lentils, which she used to prepare from any leftover stew, with extra herbs and spices, and then warm up as a snack for later in the week. I don't really know why, I simply couldn't eat it. The ingredients were the same as the lentil stew, the spices or herbs were not the problem because she used them regularly, I just had an aversion to puréed lentils. (I still don't like dahls.)

Anyway, in one of her 'puréeing sessions' she added loads of garlic, slowly pan-fried first in olive oil until it was nice and golden, and handfuls of pan-fried fresh rosemary. And the smell of the garlic and rosemary together was heavenly. So that is how this recipe came about – only we've left out the lentils and used broad beans instead.

Serve it cold or lukewarm as a dip with crusty bread. Any leftover purée can be stored in the fridge for up to 3 days.

Makes
1 litre

olive oil

8 **garlic cloves** – yes, this is a seriously garlicky dip

Maldon sea salt and **cracked black pepper**, to taste

5 sprigs **fresh rosemary** (or 1 heaped tablespoon dried rosemary)

500g **broad beans** (fresh, frozen or tinned – we use frozen, just make sure you defrost them), husks removed

Heat 4 tablespoons of olive oil in a large, heavy-based frying pan on a medium heat. Peel the garlic cloves and crush them with the flat side of a broad blade knife or the bottom of a tablespoon. Add them to the pan with a pinch of salt and pepper and stir them around in the hot oil. Turn the heat right down and sauté very gently for 15–20 minutes, or until soft and pale golden brown. Remove with a slotted spoon and place in a dish to one side.

Return the pan to a low heat, drop in the sprigs of rosemary and season with a further pinch of salt and pepper. Stir the rosemary around in the pan and fry gently until the leaves begin to change colour – about 5–7 minutes. Remove with a slotted spoon and place in the dish with the garlic. Take the pan off the heat and allow the infused oil to cool down.

When the oil is lukewarm, pour it into your food-processor and drop in the garlic, rosemary and broad beans. Set the processor off at a slow speed and blend to a thick, smooth paste. If it is too thick, add a bit more olive oil. Season to taste. Once done, spoon into a serving bowl and serve immediately, or heat up in a low oven and serve lukewarm.

Romanesco de Almendras y Pipas Tostadas

Almonds, sunflower and pumpkin seeds roasted with garlic, tomatoes, chillies and olive oil

A friend of ours, John Humphries, came in and told us about this marvellous almond paste he had tried in a restaurant in Catalonia. John is a man who knows his wine, beer, tequila and food so we immediately got to work on it. At first we just used almonds, and then one day at one of our menu meetings we thought why not add some other seeds? And this is the result.

Any leftover sauce can be stored in the fridge for 3 days. Take out what you need, spoon it into a small dish, and allow it to come up to room temperature before serving.

Makes 1 litre

10 **cherry tomatoes**

olive oil

Maldon sea salt and **cracked black pepper**, to taste

3 **garlic cloves**, peeled and crushed

1 **red chilli,** deseeded and finely chopped

250g **almonds** (skins on)

100g **sunflower seeds**

100g **pumpkin seeds**

Preheat your oven to 150°C/300°F/gas mark 2. Place the tomatoes in a roasting tray and pour over 8 tablespoons of olive oil. Season with salt and pepper, and then place in the oven for 45 minutes to 1 hour in total, stirring every so often. Half-way through their cooking, add the garlic and the chillies, then mix well.

While the tomatoes, garlic and chillies are roasting, pour 10 tablespoons of olive oil into a large, heavy-based frying pan and place on a low heat. Add the almonds and a pinch of salt and pepper, and fry them very gently for 5 minutes. Keep an eye on them because you don't want them to burn – any that do burn should be removed and discarded or they'll make the dip taste bitter. Just before the almonds turn golden brown, toss in the seeds and stir well. Continue to cook together for a further 2 minutes, and then tip the toasted nuts and seeds into the roasting tray with the tomatoes. Return the tray to the oven until the tomatoes, garlic and chillies are completely soft. Remove from the oven and leave to cool.

Once cold, place the ingredients in a food-processor and blitz on a slow setting until creamy, but not smooth. The finished sauce should be glistening with oil, but not steeped in it, and it should have the consistency of rustic pesto sauce. If it is too thick, add a little extra oil and keep blending. If it is too runny, quickly brown off some more almonds and seeds (making sure you season them) and add them to the food-processor. Serve with chunky bread, or as an accompaniment to meat or vegetable dishes.

Boquerones Adobados

Fresh marinated anchovies

As well as the three dips we serve, we have fresh, marinated anchovies that customers snack on whilst the rest of their food is prepared. Alan Davidson, in his fantastic book, *North Atlantic Seafood* points out, 'The anchovy, of which there are various species all around the world, is unique… in that it is not normally eaten fresh although it can be, but is marketed in almost every other form: salted; canned whole or filleted, in oil or sauce; hot smoked; reduced to fish sauce or to a pâté or to anchovy essence.' In England they are very difficult to come by. Sprats (from the sardine family) are the closest thing to them and because of their small size, are difficult to fillet. So, as Davidson says, one tends to look at the many ready prepared anchovy products available. You can buy them from the deli, but we find the marinade often tastes a bit tart and prefer to re-marinate ours in extra virgin olive oil, garlic and parsley, which we leave to steep for 12 hours to really bring out the flavour.

Serves 4

4 packets of **anchovies**, 130–150g each

200ml **extra-virgin olive oil**

3 **garlic cloves**, finely chopped

3 sprigs **flat-leaf parsley**, coarsely chopped

Drain the anchovies in a colander over the sink, shaking gently from side to side to encourage as much of the original marinade to drip out as possible. Leave to drain for 20 minutes.

Place the drained anchovies in a large, flat dish, pour over the olive oil and sprinkle over the chopped garlic and parsley. Mix well together so that the anchovies are evenly coated with the new ingredients, and then cover the dish with clingfilm and leave to marinate in the fridge for 12 hours minimum.

Serve as a snack on their own with some lovely bread, or use them in salads. Alternatively, chop them up and mix them into alioli (see page 11), or add them to fish sauce. The anchovies will keep in the fridge for up to 3 days.

fish and shellfish

Patrick and I like eating fish. So do lots of our customers. If you have a good fishmonger near by, fantastic; if you don't, most good supermarkets have a well-stocked fish counter. Try to use fresh fish wherever possible, especially for the simple pan-fried recipes. You'll need to read the label carefully or check with your fishmonger because some fish might look fresh but it may have been pre-frozen (this is often the case with squid and prawns). Frozen fish tends to get very 'spongy' and will lose its flavour. However, if that is all you have on offer, or in the freezer, just make sure you marry it with a flavoursome sauce.

By and large we try to cook fish as simply as possible at El Parador – that is, we clean the fish, season it with a pinch or two of sea salt, cracked pepper and olive oil, and then we whack it on a griddle or in a frying pan. Yes, I know I've oversimplified it a bit, but that is the gist. The key to preparing great fish is to make sure you match any accompanying sauce to the taste or texture of the fish. Fish that are meaty – monkfish, swordfish, tuna, cod or hake, for example – can by and large carry a rich sauce because the flavour of the fish will still come through. However, if a less 'meaty' fish is buried under a big heavy sauce then all you taste is the sauce – a balance has to be struck.

When you're cooking fish on a griddle or in a pan, always try to cook all the portions at the same time, rather than cooking in batches. This is particularly important with delicate fish, such as bream or bass, which are more likely to dry out if they are placed in the oven to keep warm. For best results, invest in a heavy griddle plate (see page 9).

Prawns, scallops and mussels are all very popular at El Parador. Scallops and mussels have to be fresh. 'Fresh prawns' as Rick Stein points out in his bible of seafood, *Rick Stein's Seafood* 'will almost always have been frozen and then defrosted at their destination. Prawns freeze well but do not travel well, chilled, which is why they are usually boiled at sea if they are not to be frozen'. So always buy a good-quality frozen prawn.

Lubina con Ensaladilla de Garbanzos

Grilled fillet of sea bass on a bed of chickpeas with spring onion
and coriander

Sea bass has a delicate, refined flavour that really needs little added to it. You'll need a pan large enough to accommodate all four fillets for this recipe, because the bass will dry out if you end up having to cook it in batches. You can also fry the fish in spicy chorizo oil instead of using olive oil. Put in seven thickish slices of chorizo into a 'dry', hot pan. When the chorizo is good and hot it will release its spicy juices. When there is enough oil, remove the chorizo and fry the fish in the oil.

Serves 4

olive oil

4 **sea bass fillets** (about 175g each)

Maldon sea salt and **cracked black pepper**, to taste

4 **lemon wedges**, to serve

for the chickpea salad

2 x 400g tins **chickpeas**

2 medium **spring onions**, washed, trimmed and finely sliced

2 sprigs **fresh coriander**, coarsely chopped

Maldon sea salt and **cracked black pepper**, to taste

olive oil

Drain the chickpeas in a colander and rinse under cold running water. Tip into a large bowl and add the finely sliced spring onions, the chopped coriander, 2 pinches of salt and pepper and 8 dashes of olive oil. Dig in with your hands and mix well, then divide the chickpea salad between the 4 plates.

Place your griddle plate (or large, heavy-based, non-stick frying pan) on a medium heat and pour in 6 dashes of olive oil. When the oil is smoking hot, put in the 4 bass fillets, skin-side down. Season with a generous pinch of salt and pepper, and then sear for 90 seconds on each side. Serve the fillets on top of the chickpea salad with a lemon wedge (or a couple) on the side.

Sardinas a la Plancha

Chargrilled sardines with cracked black pepper and sea salt

The smell of cooked sardines reminds me of my summer holidays in Spain and cooking them on a improvised barbecue on the beach made from rocks, using drift wood for burning… and some ice-cold beers. At El Parador we can cook them perfectly for you but you will have to dream up the beach.

Serves 4

8 medium **sardines**

Maldon sea salt and **cracked black pepper**, to taste

olive oil

4 **lemon wedges**, to serve

First gut the fish (or ask your fishmonger to do it for you). Lay a sardine on a chopping board and, holding it with one hand, use a sharp knife to make an incision from the base of its gills below its mouth, along its belly to just above its tail. Take the fish over to the sink and clean out its entrails completely (this is rather a messy/smelly job), then give the fish a good wash. Gut all the sardines in the same way, then dry them off on kitchen paper and place them on a large dish. Sprinkle a generous pinch of salt in the chest cavity of each sardine and rub a pinch of pepper into the skin.

Place your griddle plate, ridged-side up, on a high heat. Pour over 4 dashes of olive oil and tilt the plate backwards and forwards to spread it evenly around. When it is smoking hot, put on the sardines. Cook them until the eyes are completely cloudy. Then flip over and cook for the same length of time on the other side. You can tell when the sardines are cooked because the flesh nearest the spine will have gone a dark, browny-red.

To serve, arrange the cooked sardines on a serving platter with some lemon wedges on the side. Now close your eyes… inhale the aroma… and imagine you are eating them on a beautiful sandy beach.

Besugo con Hinojo

Chargrilled sea bream marinated with crushed fennel seeds and garlic

Similar to bass, bream has a slightly firmer texture.

Serves 4

olive oil

4 **sea bream fillets** (about 175g each)

2 large **garlic cloves**, finely sliced

1 teaspoon **fennel seeds**, crushed

Maldon sea salt and **cracked black pepper**, to taste

4 **lemon wedges**, to serve

First marinate the fish. Find a dish large enough to hold your 4 fillets and drizzle the base with 4 dashes of olive oil. Place the fillets of bream, skin-side down, in the dish and pour over 2 more dashes of olive oil, rubbing it into the flesh with your fingers. Place several slices of garlic on each fillet, along with a couple of pinches of fennel seeds and a generous pinch of black pepper. Cover the dish with clingfilm and leave to marinate in the fridge for 2 hours.

When you are ready to cook, set your griddle plate (or large, heavy-based, non-stick frying pan) on a medium heat. When it is smoking hot, put on the fish, skin-side down, and season with a pinch of salt. Cook for 90 seconds on each side. Serve immediately with lemon wedges on the side.

Cabracho a la Plancha

Chargrilled red snapper marinated with garlic, capers and tarragon

Snapper has a rich, earthy flavour and quite firm flesh that, if overcooked, can become dry.

Serves 4

4 **red snapper fillets** (about 175g each)

olive oil

2 large **garlic cloves**, finely sliced

3 sprigs **fresh tarragon**, coarsely chopped

8 small **capers**, coarsely chopped

Maldon sea salt and **cracked black pepper**, to taste

4 **lemon wedges**, to serve

First marinate the fish. Find a dish large enough to hold your 4 fillets and drizzle the base with 4 dashes of olive oil. Place the fillets skin-side down, in the dish, and pour over 2 more dashes of olive oil, rubbing it into the flesh with your fingers. Place some sliced garlic, chopped tarragon and capers on top of each fillet and season with a pinch of black pepper. Cover the dish with clingfilm and leave to marinate in the fridge for 2 hours.

When you are ready to cook, set your griddle plate (or large, heavy-based, non-stick frying pan) on a high heat. A griddle plate will take all 4 fillets, a pan will probably not – in which case, preheat your oven to 150°C/300°F/gas mark 2 so that you can keep the first couple of fillets warm while you cook the rest. When the griddle is smoking hot, place the fillets, skin-side down, add 1 pinch of salt and sear for 90 seconds if the pieces are thin, 2 minutes if they are thick. This will leave the fish slightly underdone in the middle; if you prefer it more cooked then leave it for a little longer. Using a spatula, carefully flip the fish over and cook it on the other side for the same length of time.

Arrange all 4 fillets together on a large plate, drizzle with olive oil and serve with some lemon wedges on the side.

Pez Espada a la Plancha

Chargrilled swordfish with sea salt and black pepper

When I was young, a lot of my family holidays were spent visiting my aunt and uncle in Seville. Because we were being looked after by my aunt, my father would insist on doing the food shopping. After picking up all the necessities, we would always stop off in a local bar with big arches and windows, lace curtains billowing. This is where I had my first ever taste of swordfish. They did nothing special to it – just careful seasoning with salt and pepper. You can substitute the swordfish with tuna steaks.

Serves 4

4 **swordfish steaks** (about 175g each)

olive oil

Maldon sea salt and **cracked black pepper**, to taste

4 **lemon wedges**, to serve

Place the pieces of swordfish on a large plate. Pour over 8 dashes of olive oil and sprinkle with 3 pinches of pepper and salt. Rub the seasoning into the flesh with your fingers so that both sides are evenly coated.

Set your griddle plate over a high heat, ridged-side up, but do not add any oil. When it is smoking hot, grill the pieces of fish for 10 seconds on each side (15 seconds if you prefer your fish more cooked). Serve straight away with lemon wedges on the side.

Salteado de Pez Espada con Tomatitos

Strips of swordfish pan-fried with roasted cherry tomatoes,
coriander and garlic

The light, flavoursome sauce really complements the taste and rich texture
of the swordfish.

Serves 4

12 **cherry tomatoes**

Maldon sea salt and **cracked black pepper**, to taste

garlic- and chilli-infused olive oil (see page 10)

4 **swordfish steaks** (about 150g each)

olive oil

2 **garlic cloves**, thinly sliced

2 small knobs of **butter**

3 teaspoons chopped **fresh coriander**

Preheat your oven to 150°C/300°F/gas mark 2. First roast the cherry tomatoes. Place them in a roasting tin with a generous pinch of sea salt and drizzle over a couple of dashes of chilli- and garlic-infused olive oil. Roast in the oven for 1 hour until soft. Remove from the oven and set to one side.

Cut each swordfish steak into 4 strips the length of your finger and twice its thickness. Place them in a bowl and drizzle with 6 dashes of olive oil and a pinch of salt and pepper.

Place a large heavy-based, non-stick frying pan (or wok) on a high heat to get good and hot, then add 3 dashes of olive oil. Add the sliced garlic, turning it in the pan until it starts to sizzle – it can go golden and a tad dark, but don't let it burn. Drop in the strips of swordfish and sear for 10 seconds, or until the undersides start to brown. Use a spatula to turn the pieces over and continue cooking until the flesh starts to turn pale – if you like your fish more well-cooked, continue cooking until it is pale right through (roughly a further 5 seconds).

Add the tomatoes and butter, and carefully stir the ingredients together. Season to taste. Once the butter starts to sizzle, sprinkle over the fresh coriander and serve with the bread of your choice.

Halibut con Alcaparras

Baked halibut with capers and butter

Halibut is an expensive fish to buy, but its flesh has a delicious, almost sweet flavour. Try not to overcook it or you will lose its succulent glory.

Serves 4

4 **halibut tranches** (about 175g each)

Maldon sea salt and **cracked black pepper**, to taste

olive oil

30g **butter**

10 small **capers**, coarsely chopped

5 **lemon wedges**

2 sprigs **flat-leaf parsley**, coarsely chopped

Preheat your oven to 150°C/300°F/gas mark 2. Place the fish in a large dish and season each piece with a pinch of salt and pepper.

Put a small frying pan on a low heat, pour in 2 dashes of olive oil and a generous pinch of pepper and give it a quick stir. Leave to heat up while you start cooking your fish.

Set a large, heavy-based, non-stick frying pan on a medium to high heat, pour in 6 dashes of olive oil and heat until smoking hot. Carefully lower your halibut pieces, skin-side down, into the pan and cook for 60 seconds each side then place the pan with the fish in the oven and leave for 4 minutes.

Meanwhile, the oil in the small frying pan should be getting good and hot. Drop the butter into the pan and, when it has melted, stir in the chopped capers. When the butter starts to sizzle and spit, quickly squeeze in the juice of one of the lemon wedges – this will stop the butter burning and give off a nice 'nutty' taste – and finally stir in the chopped parsley.

The halibut should now be ready. Place all the pieces of fish on a large platter, pour over the caper butter and serve with the rest of the lemon wedges.

Caballa a la Plancha

Grilled mackerel marinated with smoked, sweet paprika oil and garlic

A much underrated fish, mackerel is delicious and so good for you. If you can't get hold of fresh mackerel fillets, grey mullet (another underrated fish) will also work well with this recipe.

Serves 4

olive oil

1 teaspoon **smoked, sweet paprika**

Maldon sea salt and **cracked black pepper**, to taste

4 **mackerel fillets** (about 175g each)

2 **garlic cloves**, thinly sliced

4 **lime wedges**, to serve

In a small bowl, whisk together 7 dashes of olive oil, the paprika and a pinch of salt and pepper.

Coat a large dish with 4 dashes of olive oil. Place the mackerel fillets skin-side down, in the dish, and smear each one with a good spoonful of the paprika mixture, rubbing it in well. Evenly distribute the garlic slices over each fillet, then cover the dish with clingfilm and leave to marinate in the fridge for 2 hours.

When the time is up, put the griddle plate, ridged-side up, on a high heat. When it starts to smoke, put on the fillets, skin-side down first, and cook for 30 seconds on each side if the fillets are small, 70 seconds if they are large. Serve immediately with lime wedges on the side.

Raya del Parador

Pan-fried skate marinated with crushed caraway seeds and garlic

Skate belongs to the family of rays but has more of a pointed snout rather than the rounded head of other members of its family. Only its wings are used although, like the monkfish, there is meat around the 'cheeks' of the head. The wings have meat on both sides with the top side carrying more than the other. Its bones are soft cartilage and fan out from its body section. It has a beautiful, delicate flavour and texture; the only word of warning is that it goes off very quickly.

Serves 4

4 small **skate wings** (about 175g each) or 2 big wings chopped in half

olive oil

1 teaspoon **caraway seeds**, crushed

Maldon sea salt and **cracked black pepper**, to taste

2 **garlic cloves**, thinly sliced

4 **lemon wedges**, to serve

First marinate the fish. Find a dish large enough to hold all the pieces of skate side by side and coat the bottom with 4 dashes of olive oil. Arrange the skate inside, meaty-side down. Sprinkle over half the crushed caraway seeds, a generous pinch of pepper and half the garlic slices, then turn the pieces of fish over and do the same to the other side. Cover the dish with clingfilm and leave to marinate in the fridge for 2 hours.

You will probably have to cook the fish in batches, so preheat your oven to 150°C/300°F/gas mark 2.

Once you are ready to start cooking, place your griddle plate (or large, heavy-based, non-stick frying pan) on a medium to high heat and pour in 6 dashes of olive oil. When the oil is hot, lower in the pieces of skate (probably 2 at a time), placing them meaty-side down first. Cook for 45 seconds on the thickest side, then turn over and cook on the other side for 30 seconds. When the first batch of skate is cooked, transfer the fish to an ovenproof dish and place in the bottom of the oven to keep warm while you cook the rest. Serve with lemon wedges on the side.

Atún Salteado con Espinacas y Chicoria

Pan-fried tuna with spinach and chicory

Tuna is slightly sweet in flavour, which balances the slight bitterness of the chicory and the earthiness of the spinach.

Serves 4

4 **tuna steaks** (about 150g each)

olive oil

garlic-infused olive oil (see page 10)

Maldon sea salt and **cracked black pepper**, to taste

300g **young leaf spinach**, washed

1 small head of **chicory**, broken into bite-sized pieces

Cut each tuna steak into 4 strips the length of your finger and twice its thickness, and place in a dish. Add 6 dashes of olive oil and a generous pinch of salt and pepper and mix well together.

Put a large, heavy-based, non-stick frying pan (or wok) on a high heat and pour in 2 dashes of the garlic-infused olive oil. Put in the spinach, add a pinch of salt and turn the leaves gently until they start to wilt – you may have to do this in 2 hits, in which case you will need to clean out the pan with kitchen paper and heat up some more oil before you stir-fry the second batch. Just before the spinach releases its water, remove it from the pan and drain on kitchen paper to soak up the bitter juices.

Clean the pan with kitchen paper and return it to a high heat with 2 dashes of olive oil. When the oil is smoking hot, carefully lower in the strips of tuna and sear for 8 seconds on each side, depending on how you like your tuna cooked. We prefer it undercooked, so we wait until it just starts to change colour, but if you like yours more well-cooked, leave it for a little longer. When you are satisfied the tuna is cooked, throw in the chicory and the spinach, season to taste and then carefully stir-fry for 10 seconds. Serve immediately.

Atún a la Plancha con Lentejas

Grilled tuna marinated with chives and garlic, served with lentils, parsley and chilli oil

Tuna, like swordfish, has a lovely firm texture. In our opinion, it's best eaten slightly underdone to retain its moisture and flavour.

Serves 4

4 **tuna steaks** (about 175g each)

olive oil

Maldon sea salt and **cracked black pepper**, to taste

15 **chive strands**, finely chopped

3 large **garlic cloves**, finely sliced

8 tablespoons **Puy lentils,** washed

chilli-infused oil (see page 10)

2 sprigs **flat-leaf parsley**, finely chopped

4 **lemon wedges**, to serve

First marinate the tuna. Pour 6 dashes of olive oil into a large dish, sprinkle with 2 generous pinches of pepper, half the chopped chives and half the sliced garlic. Place the tuna steaks on top and rub a dash of oil and a pinch of pepper into the top of each steak. Evenly distribute the remaining chopped garlic and chives over the fish, then cover the dish with clingfilm and leave in the fridge to marinate for 2 hours.

Put the lentils in a large pan of salted water. Bring to the boil, then reduce the heat and simmer for 40 minutes. Drain and tip them into a large bowl. Pour in 8 dashes of chilli oil, then add 2 pinches of salt and the chopped parsley and mix everything together. Leave to stand at room temperature until you are ready to cook the fish.

Set the griddle plate on a high heat. When it is smoking hot, put on the tuna steaks, season to taste, and grill for 10 seconds on each side (15 seconds if you prefer your fish more cooked). Share out the lentils between 4 plates, topped with a tuna steak and lemon wedges on the side.

Empanadillas de Atún

Savoury tuna parcels

The 'empanada', which roughly translates as 'made from bread', is Spain's equivalent of a Cornish pasty. It usually comes in the shape of a pie, but can be shaped like a pasty or turnover. There are many fillings – fish, meat and vegetarian (see page 133).

Serves 4–6

for the filling

olive oil

2 medium **onions**, finely sliced

1 large **red pepper**, finely chopped

Maldon sea salt and **cracked black pepper**, to taste

225g **fresh tomatoes**, coarsely chopped

1 x 350g tin good-quality **tuna** (in oil), drained

8–10 good-quality **black olives**, stones removed

Small pinch of **saffron strands**, soaked in 2 tablespoons hot water

for the pastry

packet of ready-rolled **puff pastry**

1 beaten **egg**

Place a large, heavy-based, non-stick frying pan (or wok) on a low heat with 8 dashes of olive oil. Add the sliced onions and peppers, a pinch of salt and pepper, then sauté gently until soft and tender.

Add the chopped tomatoes and give everything a good stir, then simmer gently until all the ingredients have reduced to a thick sauce.

Add the tuna, olives, saffron and another pinch of salt and pepper. Simmer everything together, stirring regularly until you have a thick, rich sauce. Set aside to cool, and then refrigerate for 2 hours.

Preheat your oven to 200°C/400°F/gas mark 6.

Lightly flour your worksurface and place the rolled puff pastry on top. Using a sharp knife, cut the pastry into 12cm squares and arrange them on several greased baking sheets. You will need 8–12 depending on how many people you are serving. Gauge it so you have enough pastry to wrap the filling. If the pastry is too thin, the parcel will burst and all the ingredients will spill out. Some spillage is fine. If the pastry is too thick, it will not allow the flavours of the filling to come through.

Put a dollop of the tuna mixture, a ball shape roughly 5–6cm in diameter, in the middle of the square, and then dab the edges of the square with beaten egg. Bring up the corners of the pastry to the centre and press them together to form a peak at the top. Glaze the tops with beaten egg, and then bake in the oven for 20 minutes, or until golden brown. Serve hot, warm or cold.

Rape Salteado al Ajillo Asado y Salsa Picante

Monkfish marinated with garlic oil and parsley, pan-fried with a cherry tomato, roasted chilli, garlic and red pepper sauce

The chilli-pepper sauce can be made up in advance and stored in the fridge.

Serves 4

2 **monkfish tails** (about 275g each), skinned (including the outer membrane), filleted and cut into 12 even slices or 'medallions'

garlic-infused olive oil (see page 10)

3 sprigs **flat-leaf parsley**, coarsely chopped

Maldon sea salt and **cracked black pepper**, to taste

olive oil

for the roasted chilli and red pepper sauce

4 large **red peppers**

2 **red chillies**

5 **cherry tomatoes**

6 **garlic cloves**, peeled

olive oil

Maldon sea salt and **cracked black pepper**, to taste

First marinate the fish. Place the slices of monkfish in a bowl and pour over 12 dashes of garlic-infused oil (or enough to coat the fish). Work the oil into the flesh with your fingers, then sprinkle over the chopped parsley and a generous pinch of pepper. Mix well together, then cover with clingfilm and leave to marinate in the fridge for a minimum of 2 hours.

Now for the roasted chilli and red pepper sauce. Preheat your oven to 150°C/300°F/gas mark 2. Spike a pepper with a skewer or a long fork (or grab it with some tongs) and hold it over a high flame to blacken the skin – wear an oven glove just in case. Repeat with the remaining peppers and the chillies. Peel off the charred skin and discard. (Wrapping the peppers/chillies in clingfilm for a few minutes after charring them causes them to sweat, and this makes peeling them much easier.) Hull and deseed the chillies and peppers and place them, along with the cherry tomatoes, in a roasting tray with the 6 garlic cloves. Drizzle over 3–4 dashes of olive oil and season with salt and pepper. Place in the oven and roast slowly for 45 minutes – keep an eye on them because you don't want them to burn (any that do start to colour should be removed and placed to one side). Once everything is nice and soft, take the tray out of the oven and leave to cool. Remove the roasted garlic cloves and set aside. When the chillies and peppers are cool enough to handle, tip them with their juices into a food processor. Add a good slug of olive oil and blitz to a smooth paste. Adjust the seasoning and thin with extra olive oil, if necessary – you are aiming for a smooth paste so pour in the olive oil a little at a time. Pour into a bowl and place to one side.

Put a large, heavy-based non-stick frying pan (or wok) on a high heat. Pour 6 dashes of infused olive oil into the pan and get it nice and hot. Put in the monkfish and let each side cook for 20 seconds and season to taste. Once the flesh has turned white, pour in the pepper sauce and add the garlic. Stir in well, ensuring that the fish is coated with the sauce. Add more oil if the sauce starts to dry up. Cook for a further 30 seconds then serve.

Rape al Vino

Monkfish braised with white wine, onions, peppers and garlic

My dad once suggested the following monkfish recipe to the chefs and after much deliberation and chewing of the cud, it was tried, and enjoyed by all.

Serves 4

olive oil

1 medium **Spanish onion**, finely sliced

1 medium **green pepper**, finely sliced

2 **garlic cloves**, thinly sliced

2 **monkfish tails** (about 300g each), skinned (including the outer membrane) and filleted

2 sprigs **fresh thyme**, chopped

2 **bay leaves**

500ml **white wine**

Maldon sea salt, **cracked black pepper** and **whole black peppercorns**

generous knob of **butter**

handful of **fresh coriander**, coarsely torn

Place a large, deep frying pan on a medium heat, add 10 dashes of olive oil, the sliced onion, sliced pepper and sliced garlic and fry until golden brown. Add the 4 monkfish fillets and fry them for 30 seconds on each side, or until the flesh turns opaque. Add the chopped thyme, bay leaves, wine, a pinch of whole black peppercorns and a generous pinch of salt. Stir in the butter and simmer gently for 8–10 minutes. Carefully remove the monkfish and keep warm under foil.

Set the pan back on a fierce heat and bubble vigorously to reduce the sauce by half. Add more seasoning, if necessary. Return the fish to the pan with the fresh coriander and simmer gently for a further 5 minutes. Serve immediately.

Rape con Ajo y Espárragos del Mar

Monkfish pan-fried with garlic and samphire

Monkfish lends itself well to various cooking techniques, including frying, stewing, chargrilling and carpaccio, because of the firmness of its flesh. In this popular dish, it is pan-fried with garlic and samphire, a wild, edible plant that grows on mudflats in estuaries. Also known as sea asparagus, it has a limited season in Britain, from mid- to late summer – after that, it starts to get woody. At other times of the year, a good vegetable supplier or fishmonger should be able to source it from mainland Europe, where its season starts earlier and carries a little longer. Samphire is slightly salty in flavour, so it doesn't need any extra seasoning. A great accompaniment to fish, it is also delicious served on its own (see Espárragos del Mar con Alioli de Hinojo Asado, page 151). This recipe works equally well with fat, juicy tiger prawns (shells off) in place of the monkfish.

Serves 4

2 **monkfish tails** (about 275g each), cleaned, skinned (including the outer membrane), filleted and cut into 12 even slices or 'medallions'

3 **garlic cloves**, thinly sliced

Maldon sea salt and **cracked black pepper**

olive oil

40g **fresh samphire**, washed

First marinate the fish. Place the slices of monkfish in a bowl with the sliced garlic and 3 generous pinches of pepper. Add 5 dashes of olive oil and mix everything together. Cover with clingfilm and leave to marinate in the fridge for 2 hours.

The samphire will come in bunches or clusters. Pick out any wilted or dying pieces and separate the rest into strands.

When the fish has marinated long enough, place a large, heavy-based, non-stick frying pan (or wok) on a high heat and pour in 6 dashes of olive oil. When the oil is hot, drop in the garlicky monkfish and stir-fry the fish for 40 seconds, or until it starts to colour. Season to taste. Throw in the samphire and continue to cook, stirring, for a further 30 seconds – don't worry if the garlic blackens slightly. Serve immediately.

Salteado de Huevas de Bacalao

Cod roe pan-fried with garlic, coriander and chargrilled red peppers

Cod roe is certainly an acquired taste. We think it's delicious, and it always goes down well at El Parador.

Serves 4

olive oil

2 **garlic cloves**, thinly sliced

Maldon sea salt and **cracked black pepper**, to taste

25g **plain flour**

350g **fresh cod roes**

50g **butter**

1 large **red pepper**, chargrilled (see pages 102–3), and then cut into thin strips

2 sprigs **fresh coriander**, coarsely chopped

4 slices **French bread**, cut on the diagonal

4 **lemon wedges**, to serve

Place a large, heavy-based, non-stick frying pan (or wok) on a low heat with 12 dashes of olive oil. Drop in the garlic, season with a generous pinch of black pepper and fry gently until soft and golden. Remove the garlic with a slotted spoon and place in a dish to one side. Return the pan with the oil to a medium heat.

Sprinkle the flour onto a plate, and then lightly dust the cod roes in it ready for frying. Add the butter to the frying pan and, as it begins to sizzle, carefully lower in the cod roes. Season with 2 generous pinches of both black pepper and salt, and then fry the roes for 2 minutes on each side. Add the garlic, chargrilled peppers and fresh coriander, and continue to cook for a further 2 minutes. Meanwhile, toast the bread and drizzle with a little olive oil. Give the roes a final toss, and serve them over the bread slices with lemon wedges on the side.

Merluza Rebozada

Hake deep-fried in a light beer batter

The following dish was on our first-ever menu, 20 years ago. My dad used to cook it for us as kids, then went on to cook it for his grandchildren, and El Parador has been serving it on and off since day one. You can substitute the hake with cod, salt cod (see page 38), coley, sole, monkfish or big tiger prawns.

The beer keeps the batter light and crisp (you can use soda water, if you prefer, but in our opinion it doesn't taste as good). We use lager, but you can use stout, Guinness or ale – just bear in mind that the Guinness or any dark ale will darken the batter.

Serves 4

for the batter
240g **plain flour**
pinch of **paprika** (mild or spicy)
pinch of **turmeric**
Maldon sea salt and **cracked black pepper**, to taste
1 x 330ml can **lager** (or ale/stout)

4 thick **hake fillets** (about 150–175g each), skin on
Maldon sea salt and **cracked black pepper**, to taste
sunflower oil, for deep-frying
4 **lemon wedges**, to serve

Start by making the batter. In a large mixing bowl, combine the flour, paprika, turmeric and salt and pepper. Make a well in the centre and gradually pour in the lager, mixing thoroughly. You are trying to create a mixture thick enough to coat the fish, somewhere between single and double cream. If the mixture seems too runny, whisk in a little extra flour. If it is too thick, you'll have to crack open another can of lager – you can always drink the rest, especially if it's decent beer. To test the consistency, stick your finger into the batter – you should be able to just make out the creases in your knuckle through the coating. If necessary, strain through a sieve into a clean bowl to remove lumps. Cover with clingfilm and leave in the fridge for 30 minutes.

It is advisable to fry the 2 fillets at a time, then drain on kitchen paper and place in a preheated oven at 150°C/300°F/gas mark 2 to keep warm while you fry the rest. Place your fillets of fish on a clean plate and season with salt and pepper. Pour enough sunflower oil to cover the fish (5–6cm) into a large, deep-sided pan and get the oil smoking hot. Dip the fillets into the batter, coating them all over, and fry for 6–8 minutes in the hot oil. Serve with lemon wedges on the side.

Bacalao Rebozado

Salt cod deep-fried in a light beer batter

Another fish that goes well with the beer batter is salt cod. It is cod that has been preserved and dried out with lots of salt. For centuries, salting meats and fish was a way of preserving them for transport or storage. Salt cod was also used as a bartering commodity. It is something that will not be readily available in supermarkets so you will have to hunt down a good fishmonger, or a good Spanish/Portuguese delicatessen. The fish will be heavily salted, so it requires some advance preparation. Rub off some of the salt crust and then leave the fillets to soak in water for 24–48 hours. You will have to do two or three water changes during this period. The fish should not taste overly salty after its soaking and the only way to check this is to have a nibble. If it is acceptable then remove from the water. If it is too salty, then discard the water and refill with fresh water and carry on soaking. You will have to check it regularly as you do not want to take all the salt out of it.

As a kid, I used to come across jars of salted pork meat and bones in cupboards at home. There would be pigs' trotters, ribs, tails... all caked in a thick layer of salt. The first time I came across one, the temptation to open the jar and have a taste left me spitting and running for water. My mother would put them into soups and stews to give them flavour, then remove them before serving. That's why one of my great mates, Steve Munns, a dedicated vegetarian, had to be very careful every time he came over to eat at my house. She could not grasp what being a vegetarian meant, and would say that 'it is only there to give it some flavour'. Poor Steve, I am sure that out of politeness he had to endure a few non-vegetarian meals... bless him!

Serves 4

4 **salt cod fillets**, (about 150g each), cut into strips the length of your finger and twice its width

for the batter
240g **plain flour**
pinch of **paprika** (sweet or hot)
pinch of **turmeric**
Maldon sea salt and **cracked black pepper**, to taste
1 x 330ml can **lager** (or ale/stout)
sunflower oil, for deep-frying

Once you have removed the excess salt as above, follow the recipe for the Merluza Rebozada (page 37), using the same recipe for the batter. It is worth the hassle. It has a delicate flavour and goes great with a lovely glass of say Albarino, fino sherry or an ice-cold beer.

Tortitas de Bacalao

Salt cod pancakes

We also use salt cod to make pancakes and mini tortillas. The original recipe comes from Andalusia in southern Spain where many bars make little tortillas with shrimps and deep-fry them. My dad would make them as you would a pancake. He made them with shrimps, but his favourite, and ours, was with salt cod. He would shallow fry them, but at El Parador, we drop them on the hot griddle. If you don't have a griddle, use a heavy-based non-stick frying pan, and make sure you get the oil very hot or the tortitas will end up greasy.

Serves 8 (makes 24)

400g **salt cod**, soaked in fresh water for 24–48 hours (see page 38)

for poaching the fish
1 **celery** stick, roughly chopped
1 medium **carrot**, roughly chopped
1 small **onion**, roughly chopped
pinch **whole black peppercorns**
1 **bay leaf**

for the batter
200g **self-raising flour**
1/2 teaspoon **sweet paprika**
1/2 teaspoon **turmeric**
cracked black pepper, to taste
2 **eggs**
300ml **milk**

olive oil
2 large **garlic cloves**, finely sliced
1 medium **leek**, washed and finely sliced
50g **unsalted butter**
2 sprigs **fresh coriander**, coarsely chopped
8 **lemon wedges**, to serve

Start by poaching the soaked cod. Place it in a large pan with the poaching ingredients. Cover with cold water and bring to the boil, then turn the heat right down and simmer, uncovered, for 30 minutes. When it is cooked, drain the fish, reserving the cooking liquid, and peel away the skin. Remove the bones, and then flake the flesh into a clean bowl and set aside.

Preheat your oven to 150°C/300°F/gas mark 2. Now for the pancake batter. Combine the flour, paprika, turmeric and a couple of pinches of black pepper in a large mixing bowl. Make a well in the centre and crack in the eggs. Gradually pour in the milk, beating all the time until smooth. You can use a food-processor for this, if you wish. You are aiming for a batter the consistency of thick single cream. If the mixture is too thin, whisk in a little extra flour; if it is too thick, add a little of the fish stock. If necessary, strain through a sieve into a clean bowl to remove any unwanted lumps.

Pour 7 dashes of olive oil into a larger, heavy-based, non-stick frying pan and set on a low to medium heat. Throw in the sliced garlic and leek and caramelise until soft and golden. Add the butter and stir in until melted, then add the fish and fry for a few minutes more. Tip the contents of the pan into the bowl of batter, add in the chopped coriander and stir well.

Set a griddle plate on a high heat and pour in 3 dashes of olive oil. When the oil starts to smoke, drop a large tablespoon of the fish batter into the pan – it should spread to roughly the size of a teacup saucer. Cook for 2 minutes on each side. When the first pancake is cooked, place it in an ovenproof dish to keep warm in the oven. Then add more oil to the pan and fry the remaining tortitas in the same way. Serve with lemon wedges on the side.

Tortillitas de Bacalao

Salt cod omelettes

We think of the two recipes here, this one is our favourite.

**Serves 8
(makes 24)**

olive oil

30g **unsalted butter**

2 large **garlic cloves**, finely sliced

1 medium **leek**, washed and finely sliced

5 **eggs**

2 sprigs **fresh coriander**, coarsely chopped

Maldon sea salt and **cracked black pepper**, to taste

1/2 teaspoon **turmeric**

1/2 teaspoon **sweet paprika**

400g **salt cod**, soaked in fresh water for 24–48 hours (see page 38), then poached for 30 minutes (see opposite) and flaked into a bowl

8 **lemon wedges**, to serve

Preheat your oven to 150°C/300°F/gas mark 2. Place a large, heavy-based, non-stick frying pan on a low heat. Pour 6 dashes of olive oil into the pan. When the oil is hot, add the butter. When the butter starts to bubble, add the garlic and leeks and sauté until soft and golden. Remove with a slotted spoon and leave to one side. Leave the oil in the pan and turn the heat off.

In a large mixing bowl, beat the eggs with the coriander, a couple of pinches of pepper, a small pinch of salt, the turmeric and paprika. Add the fish, garlic and leek and stir well.

Put the pan back on a low to medium heat. Pour in 3 more dashes of olive oil. When hot, drop two, separate, ladlefuls of the egg and fish mixture into the pan and reduce the heat slightly. Cook until brown then flip it over and brown the other side. Place the cooked omelettes in an ovenproof dish to keep warm in the oven. Fry the remaining omelettes in the same way. Serve with lemon wedges on the side.

Bacalao Adobado

Fresh cod marinated with oregano, garlic, cumin, paprika and bay leaves, floured and shallow-fried

Fresh cod or hake can be used for this recipe. My mother use to make this for us all the time. It is a well known dish throughout Spain, which involves marinating the fish in vinegar and other herbs to the point of curing it, then quickly shallow-frying it. The vinegar gives it a slightly sharp initial flavour but then the rest of the ingredients come through giving the dish a more rounded, complete taste. Don't be put off by the lengthy list of ingredients; they all go in the marinade. The final cooking stage is very simple. The original recipe is called Bacalao Bienmesabe, which literally translated means 'cod really-tastes-good-to me'.

Serves 4

700g fresh **cod fillet** (skin on)

2 large **garlic cloves**, finely sliced

1 tablespoon fresh, chopped **oregano**

$1/2$ tablespoon **cumin seeds**, crushed

$1/2$ tablespoon **sweet paprika**

2 **bay leaves**

Maldon sea salt and **cracked black pepper**, to taste

500ml **white wine vinegar**

sunflower oil, for shallow-frying

1 teacup **plain flour**, for flouring the fish

4 **lemon wedges**, to serve

First marinate the cod. Spread the fillet (or fillets) on a chopping board and cut into strips, roughly the length of a fish finger but slightly thicker. Place in a large bowl. Add the sliced garlic, fresh oregano, cumin seeds, sweet paprika, bay leaves and 2 generous pinches of salt and pepper. Mix well together, and then add the vinegar. Cover with clingfilm and leave to marinate in the fridge for 24 hours.

It is advisable to fry the cod in two batches so the fish fries evenly. Keep the first batch warm in a preheated oven at 150°C/300°F/gas mark 2. When you are ready to cook, place a deep-sided pan on a medium to high heat and pour in 5–6cm sunflower oil. While your oil is heating, place the flour in a mixing bowl and gently dip the strips of fish in it so they are evenly coated. When the oil is smoking hot, carefully lower the fish into the hot oil. Fry until golden brown, and then remove with a slotted spoon and place on kitchen paper to soak up any excess oil. Sprinkle with salt and serve with lemon wedges on the side.

Puré de Papas con Pescado Ahumado

Smoked haddock fishcakes with potatoes, spring onions and coriander

We regularly put on a fishcake recipe at El Parador but by far the most popular is the one made with smoked haddock.

Serves 8

1kg **Desirée red potatoes**, peeled and cut into largish chunks

Maldon sea salt and **cracked black pepper**, to taste

75g **unsalted butter**

olive oil

700g **smoked haddock fillet**, thoroughly deboned

1 large **spring onion** (green tops removed), finely chopped

2 **garlic cloves**, finely sliced

juice of ¹/₂ **lemon**

2 sprigs **coriander**, coarsely chopped

4 **lemon wedges**, to serve

Preheat your oven to 180°C/350°F/gas mark 4. Place the potatoes in a large saucepan with 3 generous pinches of salt, cover with cold water and boil until soft. Drain, return to the pan with the butter, 2 generous pinches of black pepper and mash thoroughly. Cover with a lid and set to one side.

Pour 5 dashes of olive oil into a large roasting tin, ensuring that it coats the base. Put in the haddock, skin-side down, add the chopped spring onions and garlic and a couple of pinches of black pepper and drizzle over 4 more dashes of olive oil. Roast in the oven for 10 minutes, but keep an eye on it and stir after a few minutes to make sure the onions and garlic aren't burning. When the haddock is cooked – it may need a few more minutes if it is very thick – take it out of the oven and remove the skin. Flake the fish into a bowl and take out any bones. Turn the oven down to 150°C/300°F/gas mark 2.

Spoon the flaked fish into the potatoes and scrape in the onions/garlic, coriander and cooking juices from the roasting tin. Squeeze over the lemon juice, and mix well together. Place to one side for 10 minutes to develop the flavours. To shape the fishcakes, separate the mixture into 16 equal portions and mould into patties about the size of a burger.

You will probably have to fry the fishcakes in batches. Put your griddle plate (or large, heavy-based, non-stick frying pan) on a high heat and allow it to get smoking hot. Add 6 dashes of olive oil and fry the fishcakes until golden brown on both sides and piping hot in the middle. Transfer to a baking tray and place in the oven to keep warm while you fry the rest. Serve with lemon wedges on the side.

Puré de Papas con Caballa Ahumada

Smoked mackerel fishcakes with parsley, mint, butter and whole-grain mustard

Smoked mackerel is bursting with flavour and makes a delicious fishcake. We tend to prefer strong-flavoured fish when we make our fishcakes otherwise the potato element can swamp the whole thing.

**Serves 8
(makes 16)**

1kg potatoes **Desirée red potatoes**, peeled and cut into largish chunks

Maldon sea salt and **cracked black pepper**, to taste

75g **unsalted butter**

3 teaspoons **whole-grain mustard**

olive oil

4 **smoked mackerel fillets**, thoroughly deboned

3 sprigs **flat-leaf parsley**, coarsely chopped

3 sprigs **fresh mint**, coarsely chopped

8 **lime wedges**, to serve

Place the potatoes in a large saucepan with 3 generous pinches of salt, cover with cold water and boil until soft. Drain, return to the pan with the butter, 2 generous pinches of black pepper and the mustard and mash thoroughly. Cover with a lid and set to one side. Preheat your oven to 150°C/300°F/gas mark 2.

Pour 4 dashes of olive oil into a large, non-stick frying pan and set over a medium heat. Add 2 pinches of black pepper and, when it starts to sizzle, carefully lower in the mackerel fillets, skin-side down. Fry for about 15 seconds on each side, or until light golden brown. Remove with a slotted spoon and drain on kitchen paper. Scrape away the skin and flake the fish into a bowl. Stir in the parsley and mint, and then spoon the mixture into the pan of mashed potato. Mix everything together really well and leave to stand for 10 minutes to develop the flavours. To shape the fishcakes, separate the mixture into 16 equal portions and mould into patties about the size of a burger.

You will probably have to fry the fishcakes in batches. Put your griddle plate (or large, heavy-based, non-stick frying pan) on a high heat and allow it to get smoking hot. Add 6 dashes of olive oil and cook the fishcakes until golden brown on both sides and piping hot in the middle. Transfer to a baking tray and keep warm in the bottom of the oven while you cook the rest. Serve with lime wedges on the side.

Ensalada de Pescado Ahumado

Warm smoked haddock salad with French beans, chicory and roasted cherry tomatoes with a lemon and olive oil dressing

This is such a simple, yet flavourful salad. The ingredients all combine well together and the finished dish looks beautiful. A great summer salad.

Serves 4

garlic-infused olive oil (see page 10)

4 **smoked haddock fillets** (about 150g each)

1 head of **chicory**, broken into bite-sized pieces

15 **French beans**, trimmed and blanched in boiling water until just tender

12 **cherry tomatoes**, roasted in chilli- and garlic-infused olive oil (see page 25)

4 **lime wedges**, to serve

for the dressing

120ml **extra virgin olive oil**

juice of 1 **lemon wedge**

Maldon sea salt and **cracked black pepper**, to taste

Whisk the ingredients for the dressing together in a large bowl and season. The dressing should have a light, refreshing, lemony bite to it, but it should not be too tart. Leave to one side.

Put your griddle plate (or large, heavy-based frying pan) on a high heat. Pour in 4 dashes of garlic oil and tip the pan backwards and forwards to coat the base. When the oil is smoking hot, lower in the haddock fillets, skin-side down, and sear them for 30 seconds on each side.

Meanwhile, add the chicory, beans and roasted tomatoes to the bowl of dressing and dig in with your hands to mix well. Divide the salad between 4 serving plates.

To serve, place a haddock fillet on each pile of salad and drizzle with a little more garlic oil. Serve with lime wedges on the side.

Calamares a la Romana

Deep-fried squid rings

When people go to a restaurant for the first time and study the menu, they're invariably drawn to dishes they're familiar with – maybe ones they've tried on holiday. One dish that is always popular at El Parador is deep-fried squid, a classic Mediterranean dish. If you can find fresh squid for this dish, all the better – but it may not be easy to come by. Most squid will have been pre-frozen, so be judicious. Watch out if it has a pale pink hue to it or a strong smell – it may have been hanging around for a while.

Serves 4

6 heaped tablespoons **plain flour**

Maldon sea salt and **cracked black pepper**, to taste

1 teaspoon **paprika** (optional)

4 medium **squid** (about 18cm long in body size)

2 **lemons**, cut into wedges

4 sprigs fresh **coriander**, coarsely chopped

sunflower oil, for deep-frying

Combine the flour, some salt and pepper and the paprika (if using) in a deep bowl. The paprika gives the squid a gentle, smoky flavour. Leave to one side.

Now for the unpleasant bit – cleaning the squid. Grab hold of the body in one hand and the head section in the other. Gently pull the head from the body – it should come away pretty easily. Discard the entrails. It is very rare to find the ink sac intact – if you do, the ink can be used to enhance fish sauces and other seafood dishes. Pull out the quill-like bone that runs the length of the body and rinse out the body thoroughly. To remove the skin, pinch it with your fingertips to make a tear and then peel it off. Tear the wing parts off the body.

Cut up the body into rings the width of your little finger. Slice the wings into strips and place them, along with the rings, in a large bowl. Get the tentacles and cut the head off where it meets them. Squeeze out the beak, which should be just where you have made the cut. If the tentacles are long, cut them into 10cm strips; if they are short, keep them whole. Place the tentacles in the bowl with the rest of the cleaned squid and drop in 3 lemon wedges (don't squeeze them or it will start to 'cook' the squid). Throw in the chopped coriander and mix well. The coriander gives the dish a hint of tanginess; the unsqueezed lemon helps to tenderise the squid. Cover the bowl with clingfilm and leave to marinate in the fridge for a couple of hours.

When you are ready to cook, pour 5–6cm of sunflower oil into a large, deep-sided saucepan on a medium heat. Meanwhile, dip the pieces of squid into the bowl of seasoned flour, coating them thoroughly.

You may have to fry the squid in batches to keep the temperature of the oil up. When the oil is smoking hot, take a handful of squid, shake off any excess flour and carefully drop it into the hot oil; it will bubble up so make sure your pan is deep enough. Fry for 30–40 seconds, or until golden brown. Remove with a large slotted spoon and drain on kitchen paper, then fry up the remaining squid in the same way. Season with a couple of pinches of salt and a pinch of pepper and serve with lemon wedges on the side.

Calamares Adobados a la Plancha

Chargrilled squid marinated with garlic, chilli and coriander

For those customers who don't like deep-fried food, but like their squid, we do have alternatives.

Serves 4

4 medium **squid** (about 18cm long in body size), cleaned (see page 47) and left whole

3 **red chillies**, deseeded and finely sliced

3 large **garlic cloves**, finely sliced

2 sprigs **fresh coriander** (or flat-leaf parsley), coarsely chopped

2 **lemons**, cut into wedges

olive oil

Maldon sea salt and **cracked black pepper**, to taste

Place the squid body on a large chopping board and cut the tip off the body sac. Rip the wings off, leaving them whole, and place in a large bowl. Insert a sharp knife into the body sac and cut it open, then cut in half lengthways to give 2 pieces. Turn the pieces over and use the tip of your knife to make 4 diagonal score marks along the length of each piece of squid. Repeat, this time scoring in the opposite direction to give a cross-hatching pattern. Prepare the other bodies in the same way and place in the large bowl. If the tentacles are long, cut them into 10cm strips; if they are short, keep them whole. Add to the bowl with the rest of the squid.

To prepare the marinade for the squid, mix in the chillies, garlic, fresh coriander (or parsley), 4 lemon wedges (unsqueezed), 10 dashes of olive oil and 2 pinches of pepper. Mix well together to coat the squid, then cover with clingfilm and leave to marinate in the fridge for 12 hours.

Place your griddle plate on a high heat. Do not add oil. When it is smoking hot, place the body parts on the grill along with some of the tentacles and wings. Sprinkle with 2 pinches of salt. The squid will start to sear immediately. Let it brown almost to the point of charring. When the squid parts starts to curl up into a roll, remove and serve straight away with some lemon wedges on the side.

Salteado de Calamares con Panceta

Squid pan-fried with smoked bacon, garlic, peas and white wine

If you do not object to mixing squid and meat, then try this recipe.

Serves 4

4 medium **squid** (about 18cm long in body size), cleaned (see page 47)

2 **lemons**, cut into wedges

2 sprigs **fresh coriander**, coarsely chopped

2 **garlic cloves**, thinly sliced

olive oil

Maldon sea salt and **cracked black pepper**, to taste

3 rashers **smoked bacon**, cut into thin strips

handful of **sweet garden peas** (fresh or frozen)

100ml **white wine**

2 small knobs of **butter**

Prepare the squid and cut into bite-sized pieces (see page 47). Drop into a large bowl with 3 lemon wedges (unsqueezed), the fresh coriander and the sliced garlic. Mix everything together, then cover with clingfilm and leave to marinate in the fridge for a couple of hours.

When you are ready to cook, place a large, heavy-based frying pan (or wok) on a medium to high heat. Ideally, it would be better to cook this in one go, but if your pan is not big enough, preheat your oven to 150°C/300°F/gas mark 2 now so that you can keep the first batch warm while you cook the rest. Pour in 8 dashes of olive oil and add 2 pinches of black pepper. When the oil is hot, the pepper will start to sizzle. Stir it around, then add the bacon. Let the bacon release its flavour into the oil and, just before it starts to brown, remove it with a slotted spoon and leave to one side.

Bring the oil up to heat again, add 2 more pinches of pepper and throw in half the squid rings. Leave to sizzle for 20 seconds, then add a couple of pinches of salt, half the fried bacon and half the peas. Give everything a quick stir, then pour in half the white wine and add 1 knob of butter. Let everything bubble up fiercely for 30 seconds, then tip into an ovenproof dish, cover with foil and place in the oven to keep warm. Cook the second batch of squid in the same way. Just before you are ready to serve, add the first batch back into the pan and pan-fry quickly for 20 seconds. Serve with wedges of lemon on the side.

Chipirones en su Tinta

Baby squid pan-fried with spring onions, garlic, cherry tomatoes, coriander, squid ink and white wine

As I mentioned earlier, it is rare to find an intact ink sac, especially with baby squid that has been frozen. Even with large, fresh squid, it is more than likely that the ink sac would have been emptied by the creature in its defence, or would have burst in transport. Most of the ink used for cooking comes from cuttlefish, a close relative of squid. The only way of securing true squid ink is through your fishmonger. It comes frozen (in sachets), and chances are that they will have to order it in for you.

Serves 4

olive oil

3 **spring onions**, finely sliced

2 **garlic cloves**, finely sliced

5 **cherry tomatoes**

3 sprigs **fresh coriander**, roughly chopped

24 **baby squid** (6–10cm in length), cleaned (see page 47)

175ml **white wine**

Maldon sea salt and **cracked black pepper**, to taste

3 sachets **squid ink**

Heat 10 dashes of olive oil in a large, heavy-based frying pan (or work) on a low heat. Add the spring onions, garlic, tomatoes and coriander and cook very gently, stirring frequently, for 10 minutes. After this time, the onions should be soft and golden and the tomatoes just beginning to blister.

Add the squid, wine and a couple of generous pinches of salt and pepper. Simmer for 7 minutes, stirring all the time to coat the baby squid in the sauce. Now you have 2 choices: a classic, smooth sauce, or the El Parador version, which is slightly more rustic.

1. For a smooth sauce, remove the squid with a slotted spoon and leave to one side. Add the squid ink to the pan, increase the heat to high and cook fiercely, stirring all the time, for 5 minutes. Allow the mixture to cool slightly, and then blend in a food-processor until smooth. Return the sauce to the pan with the squid and heat through very gently for 2–3 minutes, stirring.
2. For the El Parador version, leave the squid in the pan with the other ingredients (unblended), pour over the squid ink and simmer everything gently for 5 minutes, stirring occasionally. At the last moment, turn up the heat and cook fiercely for a further 5 minutes to reduce the sauce.

Pulpo a la Parrilla

Chargrilled octopus marinated in rosemary, thyme and olive oil

You either love it or hate it. That is the relationship most people have with octopus. A staple in plenty of Spanish restaurants, if you can overcome the preparation of it – and the sight of the tentacles – it is well worth trying. When choosing octopus, ask your fishmonger for the Portuguese variety, distinguished by its reddish-brown colour, and look out for one with double rows of suckers on its tentacles, which is likely to be more tender when cooked. You may find octopus difficult to get hold of, and it can be expensive, but it is a real delicacy. Don't worry if you can only get hold of the frozen variety, however, since the cooking and marinating process will tenderise it beautifully.

Serves 4

1 **octopus** (about 750–800g)

120ml **olive oil**

2 large **garlic cloves**, thinly sliced

1 large **Spanish onion**, thinly sliced

1 large **carrot**, roughly chopped

2 sticks **celery**, roughly chopped

1 tablespoon **whole black peppercorns**

Maldon sea salt and **cracked black pepper**, to taste

600ml **white wine**

2 **bay leaves**

2 tablespoons **fresh, chopped rosemary**

2 tablespoons **fresh, chopped thyme**

Here comes the horrible part – cleaning and preparing the octopus. Turn the body of the octopus inside out and pull out all the entrails and the bone strips sticking to the body. You should be left with a hulled out body sac. Rinse out thoroughly, then re-invert the body sac and rinse again. Locate the beak, which is underneath the sac at the centre of the tentacles, and press it out, removing the soft surround as well. Some people remove the suckers and peel off some of the skin. We find this leaves the octopus looking very sterile, like a piece of rubber tubing, so we leave everything on.

Place a deep casserole dish on a medium heat and pour in 2 tablespoons of the olive oil. When it is hot, add the garlic, onion, carrot, celery and peppercorns. Let the mixture fry for a few minutes, stirring regularly. Season with salt, to taste.

Place the whole, prepped octopus into the pan and stir for a minute, then add the wine and bay leaves and bring to the boil. Reduce the heat and allow the dish to simmer gently, uncovered, for 1¹/₂–2 hours, or until the octopus is nice and tender. Remove the octopus from the casserole and place it in a large bowl to cool down.

Once the octopus is cold enough to handle, chop off the tentacles whole and cut up the body section into quarters. Place the tentacles and body section into another bowl, pour over the remaining olive oil and stir in the chopped rosemary, thyme and a little salt and pepper. Mix the ingredients well so the octopus is coated in the herby oil, cover in clingfilm and then leave to marinate in the fridge for 12 hours.

When you are ready to cook, place your griddle plate, ridged-side up, on a high heat and drizzle in a small amount of olive oil. When the oil is smoking hot, put on the octopus pieces and cook them for 2 minutes on each side if the pieces are big, or 1 minute on each side if they are small. Serve with lemon wedges on the side.

And next time you have a barbecue, bear the octopus recipe in mind – it tastes fantastic cooked over charcoal and makes a great alternative to sausages or burgers.

Carpaccio de Pulpo

Carpaccio of octopus with paprika, garlic and olive oil

> This delicious octopus recipe is a much-loved dish in all the bars in Galicia, and should be served at room temperature.

Follow the recipe opposite up to the marinating stage, adding 2 large garlic cloves (finely chopped) and 3 generous pinches of smoked paprika to the marinade. Leave to marinate in the fridge for 12 hours, taking it out an hour or so before you are ready to serve to allow it to come up to room temperature. Use a sharp knife to slice the tentacles and body parts as thinly as possible, and arrange them on a large plate. Drizzle over some of the oil from the marinade and sprinkle with a pinch of paprika. Serve with some lovely chunky bread.

Mejillones a la Marinera

Mussels with tomatoes, wine, garlic, onions and coriander

The following mussel recipe is a variation on the French classic, *moules marinière*. In Spain it is a common way of cooking mussels; we have just varied the quantities.

Serves 4

olive oil

Maldon sea salt and **cracked black pepper**, to taste

700ml **white wine**

800g **fresh mussels**, cleaned and checked

3 **garlic cloves**, thinly sliced

10 **cherry tomatoes**

1 small **onion**, thinly sliced

2 sprigs **fresh coriander**, roughly chopped

Place a large saucepan on a medium to high heat with 10 dashes of olive oil and 2 generous pinches of pepper. When the pepper starts to sizzle, pour in the wine and add 2 pinches of salt. Bring to the boil, and then add the mussels, garlic, tomatoes, onion and coriander. Cover with a lid and cook until all the mussels have opened fully (discard any that remain closed). Tip into a large serving bowl and serve with chunks of bread to soak up the sauce.

Gambas Picantes

Pan-fried tiger prawns marinated with garlic, chillies and olive oil

The firm consistency of tiger prawns means they can hold their own flavour when matched with other strong ones. In this case, the upfront flavours of the garlic and the chillies balance each other out and still allow the intrinsic flavour of the prawn to come through.

Serves 4

12 **uncooked tiger prawns** (defrosted if frozen), with shells on and heads off
olive oil
3 **garlic cloves**, thinly sliced
3 **red chillies**, deseeded, thinly sliced
Maldon sea salt and **cracked black pepper**, to taste
30g **butter**
4 **lemon wedges**

First marinate the prawns. With a sharp knife, carefully make an incision along the back of each prawn from the neck to the tail. Remove the dark line that runs along the spine. Place them in a large bowl with 150ml of olive oil, the garlic, chillies and 3 pinches of pepper. Combine well, and then cover with clingfilm and leave to marinate in the fridge for 12 hours.

When you are ready to cook, turn your grill onto high, or preheat your oven to 220°C/425°F/gas mark 7.

Place a large, heavy-based, non-stick frying pan on a high heat (you're going to be putting the pan under the grill or in the oven, so make sure it doesn't have a plastic handle). Pour in 2 dashes of olive oil and tip the pan backwards and forwards to coat the base. When it is smoking hot, drop in the prawns, along with the garlic and chillies, add a generous pinch of salt and cook for 60 seconds turning them so they all cook evenly. When the shells start to turn from green to pink, drop in the butter and stir it around so it melts, and then place the pan under the grill or in the oven for 30 seconds. Serve straight away with lemon wedges on the side.

Gambas Anisadas

Tiger prawns marinated with garlic, tarragon and olive oil, pan-fried with Anis Seco

The sweet aniseed flavours of the tarragon and the liqueur blend with the saltiness of the prawns, butter and olive oil to strike a lovely balance. It is then cut through by the garlic, with its nutty overtones.

Serves 4

12 **uncooked tiger prawns** (defrosted if frozen), with shells on and heads off
olive oil
3 **garlic cloves**, thinly sliced
3 sprigs **fresh tarragon**, coarsely chopped
Maldon sea salt and **cracked black pepper**, to taste
50ml **Anis Seco**
30g **butter**
4 **lemon wedges**, to serve

Follow the Gambas Picantes recipe (see page 58) but replace the chillies with the tarragon. Get your pan good and hot. Once you have dropped in the prawns, along with the garlic and tarragon, add a generous pinch of salt and cook for 30 seconds turning them so they all cook evenly. Pour in the Anis – be very careful because the alcohol will ignite – and cook for a further 30 seconds. Drop in the butter and stir it around so it melts, and then place the pan under the grill or in the oven for 30 seconds. Serve straight away with lemon wedges on the side.

Gambas al Romero

Pan-fried tiger prawns marinated with rosemary, garlic and olive oil

I have always associated rosemary as a herb that complements meats and it never occurred to me that it would work with seafood until one day Cob put it with some prawns.

Serves 4

12 **uncooked tiger prawns** (defrosted if frozen), with shells on and heads off
olive oil
3 **garlic cloves**, thinly sliced
3 sprigs **fresh rosemary**
Maldon sea salt and **cracked black pepper**, to taste
30g **butter**
4 **lemon wedges**, to serve

Follow the Gambas Picantes recipe (see page 58) but replace the chillies with the rosemary.

Vieiras Salteadas

Grilled scallops marinated with garlic, chilli oil and tarragon with wilted spinach and butter

Scallops have a delicate flavour and so care should be taken not to over-whelm them. The sweetness of the tarragon and the earthiness of the spinach combine to keep the garlic and chilli in check.

Serves 4

12 large **scallops** (off the shell)

chilli-infused olive oil (see page 10)

2 **garlic cloves**, thinly sliced

2 sprigs **fresh tarragon**, coarsely chopped

Maldon sea salt and **cracked black pepper**, to taste

olive oil

300g **young leaf spinach**, washed

30g **butter**

4 **lime wedges**, to serve

First marinate the scallops. Pour 120ml of chilli oil into a large mixing bowl and drop in the scallops, garlic, tarragon and 2 generous pinches of pepper. Combine well, cover with clingfilm and leave to marinate in the fridge for 2 hours.

When you are ready to cook, preheat your oven to 150°C/300°F/gas mark 2. Place a large, heavy-based pan (or wok) on a high heat with 2 dashes of olive oil. When the oil is smoking hot, put in the spinach, add a pinch of salt and turn the leaves gently in the pan until they start to wilt. Just as the spinach starts to release its water, remove the pan from the heat and tip the spinach into a bowl lined with kitchen paper to soak up the bitter cooking juices. (If your pan isn't big enough, you may have to cook the spinach in 2 hits, in which case make sure you wipe out the pan, re-oil it and get the oil good and hot before you add the second lot of spinach.) Transfer the spinach into an ovenproof dish, cover with foil and place in the bottom of the oven to keep warm.

Meanwhile, rub the butter all over the base of a clean, large, heavy-based, non-stick frying pan and place over a high heat. When the pan is smoking hot, drop in the scallops with their marinade and season each one with a small pinch of salt. Sear for 2 minutes on each side.

To serve, divide the spinach between 4 serving plates, place 3 scallops on top of each and pour over the butter from the pan. Garnish with a lime wedge on the side.

Vieiras con Puré de Calabazas

Grilled scallops marinated with garlic, coriander and chives served with roast butternut squash and pinenut mash

I often see scallops served in restaurants on a bed of some puréed vegetable: pea and mint… fennel… and chickpea. The creaminess of the squash really goes well with the similar, creamy texture of the scallops and the juices formed by the scallops, garlic, coriander and chives all melt into the squash.

Serves 4

12 large **scallops** (off the shell)

chilli-infused olive oil (see page 10)

3 **garlic cloves**, thinly sliced

2 sprigs **fresh coriander**, coarsely chopped

10 **chive** strands, finely chopped

Maldon sea salt and **cracked black pepper**, to taste

2 medium **butternut squash**, peeled and cut into quarters

1 heaped tablespoon **pinenuts**

70g **butter**

extra virgin olive oil

4 **lemon wedges**, to serve

First marinate the scallops. Pour 120ml chilli oil into a large mixing bowl and drop in the scallops, garlic, coriander, chives and 2 generous pinches of pepper. Combine well, and then cover with clingfilm and leave to marinate in the fridge for 2 hours.

When you are ready to cook, preheat your oven to 230°C/450°F/gas mark 8. Place the pieces of squash in a roasting tray, drizzle over enough chilli oil to coat them and sprinkle with 3 generous pinches of pepper and 2 of salt. Roast in the oven for 50 minutes, or until soft and just starting to brown. One minute before they are ready, stir in the pinenuts and return the tray to the oven. Once done, remove the tray from the oven and leave to one side.

Meanwhile, place the remaining 40g butter in the tray with the roasted squash and pinenuts. Stir it around so that it melts, and then mash the squash with the back of a fork to a coarse mixture.

To cook the scallops, first rub 30g butter over the base of a large, heavy-based, non-stick frying pan and place on a high heat. When it is sizzling hot, drop in the scallops, along with their marinade, and sear them for 2 minutes on each side.

To serve, dollop some of the mashed squash on 4 serving plates, place 3 scallops on top of each, pour over the butter from the pan and drizzle with some extra virgin olive oil. Garnish with a lemon wedge on the side and serve immediately.

meat and poultry

We all have our favourite meats. Cob likes pork, Hamdi likes lamb, Patrick likes... everything and I like beef. Simplicity of the dish is always the key. All of the meats we four enjoy have their specific flavours that can be enhanced by sauces, marinades, herbs and spices, how they are cooked and how long they are cooked for. Buying free range or organic is always preferable, but if not available then ask your butcher where he has sourced his meat. The same goes for supermarkets. Fresh produce has to be a first choice, but if you only have frozen produce available then think about how you will be cooking that particular type of meat. Frozen meat tends to be very tough, so steer away from grilling or pan-frying and use it more in stews or for braising.

Chicken is a much-loved meat. It can be grilled, stewed, smoked, fried... the list goes on. We usually have either a grilled or sautéed piece of chicken on the menu, adding on a stew in the colder months to keep everyone warm. Chicken breast meat always seems to be preferred by customers, although grilled breast meat tends to be a bit dry because it is so lean and there is no fat for the meat to draw moisture from. We tend to cook it with other ingredients to liven it up a bit. The darker meat of the chicken is the one we find more interesting – thighs, drumsticks, wings, livers and the 'nuggets' or 'oysters' of meat you find on the chicken's back just a bit further down from its neck. Although you can't cook them specifically, they are well worth searching out after a Sunday roast chicken fest. Also take advantage of the chicken carcass to make chicken stock (see page 9), which is always handy to have around to add to stews, casseroles and paellas to give them extra flavour.

Solomillo con Alcachofas

Strips of steak pan-fried with marinated artichoke hearts, spring onions and black pepper

Most delicatessens stock a selection of good-quality, tinned or bottled artichokes hearts. Try and get ones that haven't been steeped in anything too acidic, avoiding anything that's been previously chargrilled or mixed with other ingredients. The long-stemmed varieties are the best.

Serves 4

4 **marinated artichoke hearts** (leaf tips trimmed), cut into quarters

2 large **garlic cloves**, finely chopped

extra virgin olive oil, for the artichokes

Maldon sea salt and **cracked black pepper**, to taste

4 **fillet steaks** (about 250g each, cut into strips the length and thickness of your finger)

olive oil, for cooking

2 medium **spring onions**, finely sliced

First prepare the artichoke hearts. Place your griddle plate, ridged-side up, on a high heat. When it's smoking hot, put on the artichoke quarters and let them char until the ridge marks are heavily defined on both sides – press down on them with a spatula, if it helps. Transfer the charred artichokes to a bowl with the chopped garlic, 7 dashes of extra virgin olive oil and 2 pinches of pepper and salt. Mix well, cover the bowl with clingfilm and leave in the fridge to marinate for 2 hours.

In another bowl, combine the slices of steak with 2 pinches of black pepper and salt, cover and place in the fridge.

Preheat your oven to 150°C/300°F/gas mark 2. When you are ready to cook, place a large, heavy-based, non-stick frying pan (or wok) on a low heat and pour in 8 dashes of olive oil. Drop in the slices of spring onion and fry gently until golden brown. Remove with a slotted spoon and leave to one side. Turn the heat up to high and put in half the marinated artichokes. Fry for 30 seconds, then add half the steak and stir-fry for a further 30 seconds. Remove the steak and artichokes with a slotted spoon, transfer them to an ovenproof dish, cover with foil, and place in the oven to keep warm while you cook the rest of the meat/artichokes. Just before the second batch is ready, return the first batch to the pan along with the fried spring onions and combine everything together for a further 15 seconds. Serve immediately.

Solomillo con Ajo y Pimienta Negra

Strips of fillet steak pan-fried with black pepper, olive oil and garlic

I was in Barcelona a while ago and my family and I went to a great restaurant called Paco Meralgo, on the corner of Muntaner and Corsica. A friend of mine pointed out that if you split the name to read 'pa comer algo', it translates as 'to eat something'. Whatever way you look at the name, it's a great restaurant, serving fantastic food. This is their dish.

Serves 4

4 **fillet steaks** (about 250g each), cut into strips the length and thickness of your finger

Maldon sea salt and **cracked black pepper**, to taste

3 large **garlic cloves**, thinly sliced

olive oil

First marinate the meat. Put the steak strips into a large bowl. Add 6 pinches of black pepper, the sliced garlic and 8 dashes of olive oil. Mix the ingredients together so the meat is well coated and place in a sealed container. Leave to marinate in the fridge for 2 hours.

When you are ready to cook, preheat your oven to 150ºC/300ºF/gas mark 2. Place a large, heavy-based frying pan (or wok) on a high heat to get nice and hot. When it is smoking, add 2 dashes of olive oil and a generous pinch of black pepper. When the pepper starts to sizzle, add half the sliced steak and a generous pinch of salt. If you like your meat medium-rare to rare, sear the meat for 30 seconds, turning it throughout. If you want it more well done, leave it for a little longer (keep an eye on the garlic because you don't want it to burn). Once the meat is cooked, spoon into an ovenproof dish, cover with foil, and place in the oven to keep warm. Fry the rest of the steak in the same way, then, just before the second batch is ready, return the first batch to the pan and toss everything together for 5 seconds. Serve straight away with the bread of your choice to soak up the garlicky, peppery sauce.

Solomillo con Tomatitos Asados

Strips of steak pan-fried with roasted cherry tomatoes, black pepper, garlic, port and balsamic vinegar

This is our version of the previous recipe. It delivers the same garlic and pepper hit, but is balanced by the sweet, aromatic juices of the roasted tomatoes, balsamic vinegar and port.

Serves 4

4 **fillet steaks** (about 250g each) cut into strips the length and thickness of your finger)

Maldon sea salt and **cracked black pepper**, to taste

3 **garlic cloves**, thinly sliced

olive oil

12 **cherry tomatoes**, roasted in olive oil and salt at 150°C/300°F/gas mark 2 for 1 hour, or until soft

balsamic vinegar

50ml **ruby port**

First marinate the meat. Put the steak strips into a large bowl. Add 4 generous pinches of black pepper, the sliced garlic and 8 dashes of olive oil. Mix the ingredients together so the meat is well coated and place in a sealed container. Leave to marinate in the fridge for 2 hours.

When you are ready to cook, preheat your oven to 150°C/300°F/gas mark 2. Place a large, heavy-based frying pan (or wok) on a high heat and add 2 dashes of olive oil and a pinch of black pepper. Let the pepper sizzle, then add half the steak and a pinch of salt. Sear the meat for 20 seconds, turning it throughout. Add half the roasted tomatoes, a dash of balsamic and half the port. Stir-fry for a further 10 seconds, then spoon into an ovenproof dish, cover with foil, and place in the oven to keep warm. Fry the rest of the ingredients in the same way, then, just before the second batch is ready, return the first batch to the pan and toss everything together for 5 seconds. Serve straight away.

Montaditos de Solomillo

Open sandwiches of fillet steak, marinated with garlic, lemon and oregano

The oregano in this recipe can be substituted by marjoram or thyme.

Serves 4

4 **fillet steaks** (about 250g each)

olive oil

2 large **garlic cloves**, thinly sliced

1 teaspoon **fresh oregano**

Maldon sea salt and **cracked black pepper**, to taste

juice of 1/2 **lemon**

4 slices **French bread**, cut on the diagonal

Stretch a sheet of clingfilm over a large chopping board. Place 2 of the steaks on top and cover with another sheet of clingfilm. Bash each steak with a meat mallet (or rolling pin) until roughly the size of a teacup saucer. Repeat with the remaining steaks, then transfer to a large dish. Cover with 9 dashes of olive oil, the sliced garlic, fresh oregano, 2 generous pinches of pepper and salt and the lemon juice. Turn the steaks over a few times to ensure they are evenly coated, and then cover the dish with clingfilm. Leave to marinate in the fridge for 2 hours.

When you are ready to cook, place your griddle plate, ridged-side up, on a high heat. Meanwhile, toast the bread. When the griddle is smoking hot, lay the steaks on top and sear for 10 seconds on each side if you want your steak rare, or longer if you like your steak more well done. To serve, transfer each steak onto its piece of toast and eat immediately.

Potaje de Invierno

Beef stew with lentils, fennel, carrots, onions, red wine, garlic and chilli

This hearty stew is just what you need on a cold day – a beautiful winter warmer.

Serves 4

olive oil

3 **garlic cloves**, thinly sliced

1 medium **onion**, thinly sliced

2 medium **carrots**, peeled and cut into slices 1.5cm thick

1 head **fennel**, cut lengthways into long slivers

12 **cherry tomatoes**

1 medium **red chilli**, deseeded and thinly sliced

knob of **butter**

300g **braising steak**, cut into chunks 3–4cm square

100g **puy lentils**, washed

Maldon sea salt and **cracked black pepper**, to taste

175ml **red wine**

100ml **vegetable stock** (or water)

Place a large casserole dish on a low heat with 12 dashes of olive oil. When it is hot, add the garlic, onion, carrots, fennel, tomatoes, chilli and butter. Fry the vegetables very gently until the garlic and onion are golden and translucent. Remove the vegetables with a slotted spoon and leave to one side.

Return the casserole to a high heat and sear the steak on all sides. Turn down the heat to medium, and return the cooked vegetables to the pan with the lentils. Cook together for 20 seconds, stirring all the time, and then season with 2 pinches of salt and 1 of pepper. Pour over the wine and stock/water. Bring everything to the boil, and then turn down the heat to low, cover and simmer gently for 1½ hours. Serve straight away.

Pollo Salteado con Romanesco

Strips of chicken pan-fried with caramelised red onions and Romanesco

The Romanesco sauce complements the chicken so well in this recipe.

Serves 4

olive oil

Maldon sea salt and **cracked black pepper**, to taste

2 small **red onions**, thinly sliced

knob of **butter**

3 skinless **chicken breasts** (about 200g each), cut into strips the length and thickness of your finger

3 level tablespoons **Romanesco sauce** (see page 13)

Preheat your oven to 150°C/300°F/gas mark 2. Place a large, heavy-based frying pan (or wok) on a low to medium heat and pour in 10 dashes of olive oil. When it's hot, add 2 pinches of black pepper. Once the pepper starts to sizzle, add the sliced onions and butter and sauté gently until soft, stirring regularly. Remove the onions with a slotted spoon and leave to one side. Return the pan to a medium heat.

Add 6 dashes of olive oil. When the oil is smoking hot, add half the chicken strips and 2 pinches of salt. Fry fiercely for 1 minute (by which time the chicken should be browned), then flip over and brown on the other side. Transfer the chicken to an ovenproof dish, cover with foil, and then place in the oven to keep warm while you fry the next batch. Just before the second batch is ready, return the first batch to the pan with the cooked onions. Give everything a good stir, then adjust the seasoning and heat through for a further 30 seconds. Serve immediately with a dollop of Romanesco over the top.

Pollo al Estragón a la Plancha

Chargrilled chicken marinated with garlic, tarragon and black olives

Here is a lovely recipe for you chicken breast lovers.

Serves 4

olive oil

2 large **garlic cloves**, thinly sliced

3 sprigs **fresh tarragon**, coarsely torn

25 good-quality **black olives**, pitted and coarsely chopped

Maldon sea salt and **cracked black pepper**, to taste

4 skinless **chicken breasts** (about 200g each)

4 **lime wedges**, to serve

First marinate the chicken. In a large bowl, combine 6 dashes of olive oil with half the garlic, tarragon and olives. Sprinkle over 2 pinches of salt and pepper.

Spread a sheet of clingfilm over a large chopping board and place 2 chicken breasts on top. Cover with a second sheet of clingfilm and bash each chicken breast evenly with a meat mallet (or rolling pin). Place the chicken in the bowl with the marinade and repeat with the remaining breasts. Now pour 6 more dashes of olive oil over the top, along with the remaining garlic, tarragon and olives. Sprinkle over 2 more pinches of salt and pepper, cover the bowl with clingfilm and leave to marinate in the fridge for 12 hours.

When you are ready to cook, place your griddle plate, ridged-side up, on a high heat. When it is smoking hot, put on the chicken breasts (along with the tarragon, garlic and olives from the marinade) and chargrill for 3 minutes on each side. Serve straight away with lime wedges on the side.

Pollo a la Plancha

Grilled chicken thighs marinated with harissa, garlic and lemon

Thigh meat is incredibly succulent, but you can use breast meat if you wish. Just bash it out a bit more and chargrill it for 3 minutes on each side.

Serves 4

8 **chicken thighs** (skin on), boned – your butcher will be able to do this for you

2 tablespoons **harissa paste** (see page 11)

2 **garlic cloves**, finely sliced

juice of 1/2 **lemon**

olive oil

Maldon sea salt and **cracked black pepper**, to taste

4 **lemon wedges**, to serve

Stretch out a piece of clingfilm on a large chopping board, open out 2 of the boned thighs and place them on top. Cover with another piece of clingfilm and bash each one with a meat mallet (or rolling pin) until it's roughly a third larger than it was originally. Repeat with the remaining thighs and transfer to a large mixing bowl.

Add the harissa, sliced garlic, lemon juice, 12 dashes of olive oil, 2 generous pinches of salt and 1 of pepper. Mix everything together to ensure the chicken pieces are well coated. Cover the bowl with clingfilm and leave to marinate in the fridge for 12 hours.

When you are ready to cook, preheat your oven to 150°C/300°F/gas mark 2. Place your griddle plate, ridged-side up, on a high heat. When it starts to smoke, put 4 chicken thighs on top, skin-side down. Chargrill for 4 minutes on each side – thigh meat tends to be slightly pinker than breast meat, but don't let this put you off because it's incredibly succulent. If you find it's too pink, cook for an extra minute, but take care not to burn it. When you are satisfied the chicken is cooked, transfer it to an ovenproof dish, cover with foil, and place in the oven to keep warm while you cook the remaining pieces. Serve with lemon wedges on the side.

Pollo con Cúrcuma, Ajo, Espinacas y Cebollas

Strips of chicken marinated in turmeric and garlic, pan-fried with spinach and red onions

Turmeric is an aromatic and warm spice that gives food a rich golden colour. It complements lamb and other red meats very well, but it also works with chicken. Like saffron (its expensive cousin), it can be quite bitter and 'metallic' tasting if used in a heavy-handed way.

Serves 4

3 skinless **chicken breasts** (about 200g each), cut into strips the length and thickness of your finger

2 large **garlic cloves**, thinly sliced

1/2 teaspoon **turmeric**

olive oil

Maldon sea salt and **cracked black pepper**, to taste

2 small **red onions**, thinly sliced

250g fresh, **young leaf spinach**, washed

First marinate the chicken. Place the chicken strips in a large bowl. In a separate, small bowl, combine the sliced garlic, turmeric, 12 dashes of olive oil, 2 generous pinches of salt and 3 pinches of pepper. Add this to the chicken and dig in with your hands to ensure that the chicken is well coated. Transfer to a sealed container and leave to marinate in the fridge for 12 hours.

For best cooking results, you will have to fry the chicken in two batches to ensure it is evenly done. When you are ready to cook, place a large, heavy-based frying pan (or wok) on a low heat with 2–3 dashes of olive oil and a pinch of salt and pepper. Add the onion slices and sauté gently until soft and golden. Remove from the heat and leave to one side.

Return the same pan to a medium heat with 2 more dashes of olive oil. When the oil is hot, put in the spinach and a pinch of salt. Stir-fry quickly until the spinach starts to wilt and begins to release its water, and then tip it into a bowl lined with kitchen paper to soak up the bitter cooking juices. (If your pan isn't big enough, you may have to cook it in 2 hits, in which case make sure you wipe out the pan, re-oil it and get the oil good and hot before you add the second lot of spinach.)

Clean the pan with water and put it back on a medium to high heat with 4 dashes of olive oil. When the oil is smoking hot, drop in half the chicken strips and fry them until rich, golden brown on both sides. The slices are quite small, so this should only take a minute or two – don't worry if the garlic starts to blacken, just don't let the chicken char. Once the first batch is done, transfer the chicken to a dish while you stir-fry the second batch. When the second batch is nearly ready, return the first batch to the pan along with 2 more dashes of olive oil, the wilted spinach and the cooked onions. Heat through for 30 seconds, turning regularly, and serve.

Pollo en Pepitoria

Chicken stew with beer, almonds and garlic

I think it's safe to say that everyone likes a good chicken stew. Out of all the meats, chicken is the 'universal pleaser'. Whenever my mum made a chicken stew, she used to love having Patrick over for lunch or dinner because he would eat everything – I mean everything, bones and all! My mum would always use chicken legs or thighs – and, because she cooked the meat slowly, the bones would always be soft and juicy. I always stopped at the bones. I know I probably was, and still am, missing out, but I just don't chew bones. My favourite chicken stew is with beer and almonds, whereas Patrick prefers the classic chicken in wine and garlic (see page 79). You can substitute the chicken for pork meatballs (see page 98). Whatever the ingredients, they all follow the same method.

Serves 4

1 teacup **plain flour**, for flouring the chicken pieces

8 **chicken thighs or drumsticks** (skin on or off, your choice)

olive oil

15 **almonds** (skinned)

4 **garlic cloves**, peeled and crushed

2 x 330ml cans **lager** (or stout or ale, if you wish)

3 **bay leaves**

Maldon sea salt and **cracked black pepper**, to taste

tomato purée

Place the flour in a large bowl, drop in the chicken thighs or drumsticks and flour them lightly on all sides – this dusting will stop them sticking to the pan and the flour will thicken the sauce.

Place a large casserole dish on a low heat and pour in 10 dashes of olive oil. When it's hot, put in the almonds and let them brown. You will have to keep a close eye on them, because they'll brown very quickly – don't let any of them burn. Remove them with a slotted spoon and leave to one side to cool. Once cold, grind them in small batches in a mortar, leaving them quite coarse.

Return the pan to the heat, put in the crushed garlic and fry gently until golden brown. Remove from the pan and place with the ground almonds.

Return the pan to a medium heat, drop in 4 pieces of floured chicken and fry until golden brown all over. Remove with a slotted spoon, and then fry the remaining chicken pieces in the same way. When all the chicken is done, return it to the pan and pour over enough beer to cover. Add the bay leaves, 2 generous pinches of salt and pepper and bring to the boil. Squeeze in a generous squirt of tomato purée, put on a lid, and turn down the heat to a gentle simmer. Cook for 60–80 minutes.

About 20 minutes before you are ready to serve, stir in the ground almonds and garlic, and adjust the seasoning. If the sauce looks a bit thin, thicken it now by dissolving a spoonful of flour in a cup of cold water and whisking it into the pan. If the sauce seems too thick, thin it with a little water. Finish cooking for the last 20 minutes with the lid off.

You can either eat the stew straight away or, if you can bear to wait, allow it to cool, place the stew in the fridge to mature for 24 hours and reheat it the next day. Any leftover sauce can be stored in the fridge for 2–3 days and used as a base for a rich gravy, or added to potato and vegetable soup, or dolloped over some crushed, roasted new potatoes.

Pollo al Ajillo

Chicken stewed in wine and garlic

This is another dish that can be made up the day before and kept in the fridge for 24 hours to really intensify the flavours.

Serves 4

1 teacup **plain flour**, for flouring the chicken pieces

olive oil

5 **garlic cloves**, finely sliced

8 **chicken thighs or drumsticks** (skin on or off, your choice)

Maldon sea salt and **cracked black pepper**, to taste

750ml **dry white wine**

2 **bay leaves**

Place the flour in a large bowl, drop in the chicken thighs or drumsticks and flour them lightly on all sides – this dusting will stop them sticking to the pan and the flour will thicken the sauce.

Place a large casserole dish on a low heat and pour in 10 dashes of olive oil. Drop in the garlic slices and cook very gently until tender and golden – don't let them burn, so keep stirring them. Remove with a slotted spoon and leave to one side.

Return the pan to a medium to high heat, drop in 4 pieces of floured chicken and cook until golden brown on all sides. Remove with a slotted spoon, and then fry the remaining chicken pieces in the same way. When all the chicken is done, return it to the pan with 2 generous pinches of salt and pepper and the wine. Top up with enough cold water to cover the chicken completely. Drop in the bay leaves and the fried garlic and bring to the boil, put on a lid and turn down the heat to a gentle simmer. Cook for 60–80 minutes.

About 20 minutes before you are ready to serve, taste the sauce and adjust the seasoning. If the sauce looks a bit thin, thicken it now by dissolving a spoonful of flour in a cup of cold water and whisking it into the pan. If the sauce seems too thick, thin it with a little water. Finish cooking for the last 20 minutes with the lid off.

Pollo con Pimientos Rojos

Chicken with red peppers, wine, cumin, coriander and chickpeas

The peppers in this recipe take on an almost creamy texture after they have been gently fried and then slowly braised along with the other ingredients. All the ingredients come through, each doing their bit to make this a delicious stew.

Serves 4

1 teacup **plain flour**, for flouring the chicken pieces

olive oil

2 medium **red peppers**, finely sliced

2 **garlic cloves**, finely sliced

8 **chicken thighs or drumsticks** (skins on)

750ml **white wine**

Maldon sea salt and **cracked black pepper**, to taste

2 **bay leaves**

1/2 teaspoon **cumin seeds**, crushed

1/2 teaspoon **coriander seeds**, crushed

1 x 400g **tin chickpeas**, drained

2 sprigs **fresh coriander**, coarsely chopped

Place the flour in a large bowl, drop in the chicken thighs or drumsticks and flour them lightly on all sides – this dusting will stop them sticking to the pan and the flour will thicken the sauce.

Put a large casserole dish on a low heat and add 10 dashes of olive oil. Add the sliced peppers and garlic and sauté very gently until soft and golden. Remove with a slotted spoon and leave to one side.

Return the pan to a medium to high heat, drop in 4 pieces of floured chicken and cook until golden brown on all sides. Remove with a slotted spoon, and then fry the remaining chicken pieces in the same way. When all the chicken is done, return it to the pan, pour in the wine and enough cold water to cover. Add 2 generous pinches of salt and pepper, the bay leaves, the crushed cumin and coriander seeds and the sautéed peppers and garlic. Bring to the boil, put on a lid, and turn down the heat to a gentle simmer. Cook for 60–80 minutes.

About 20 minutes before you are ready to serve, stir in the chickpeas and the chopped fresh coriander. Adjust the seasoning and thicken the sauce, if necessary (by dissolving a spoonful of flour in a cup of cold water and whisking it into the pan). Finish cooking with the lid off. Serve straight away, or reheat the following day.

Pinchitos de Pollo

Chicken skewers marinated with cumin, coriander and garlic

The following recipe is taken from the classic recipe, 'Pinchitos Morunos'. Pork meat is usually used, but the strong North African flavours of the cumin and coriander work just as well with chicken.

Serves 4

3 skinless **chicken breasts** (about 200g each), cut into bite-size pieces

1 teaspoon **cumin seeds**, crushed

1 teaspoon **coriander seeds**, crushed

3 **garlic cloves**, finely sliced

olive oil

Maldon sea salt and **cracked black pepper**, to taste

2 **limes**, cut into quarters

8 **wooden skewers**, 12–14cm long

First marinate the chicken. Place the chicken strips in a large bowl with the cumin, coriander, garlic, 12 dashes of olive oil and 3 generous pinches of pepper and 2 of salt. Drop in 4 lime quarters (unsqueezed). Mix everything together so the chicken is coated in the oil and spices, and then cover with clingfilm and leave to marinate in the fridge for 12 hours.

When you are ready to cook, place your griddle plate, ridged-side up, on a high heat with 3 dashes of olive oil. Meanwhile, divide the marinated chicken pieces between your wooden skewers. When the oil is smoking hot, put on the skewers and 'grill' them for 2 minutes on each side. Serve with lime wedges on the side.

Higadillos Salteados

Fresh chicken livers pan-fried with serrano ham, garlic, cream sherry and balsamic vinegar

The garlic, cream sherry and butter add an extra creamy texture to the richness of the livers. Then the saltiness of the ham and the slight sharpness of the balsamic come into play, which prevents the whole dish from becoming too rich.

Serves 4

500g **fresh chicken livers**, cleaned

olive oil

Maldon sea salt and **cracked black pepper**, to taste

2 **garlic cloves**, thinly sliced

balsamic vinegar

125ml **rich cream sherry**

2 small knobs **butter** (optional)

3 thin slices **jamon serrano**, cut into fine strips

Trim away any fat from the livers and remove the sinewy vessel that runs through the middle. Marinate the livers: cut the livers in half and put them in a large bowl. Add 8 dashes of olive oil, 2 pinches of pepper and the slices of garlic. Mix well, cover with clingfilm and leave to marinate in the fridge for 2 hours.

You will have to fry the liver in 2 batches to avoid 'boiling' rather than searing the meat, so have an ovenproof dish ready and preheat your oven to 150°C/300°F/gas mark 2.

Place a large, heavy-based frying pan on a high heat. When it starts to smoke, drop in half the liver and toss it around in the pan for 90 seconds – it will start to release its bloody juices. Add 2 pinches of salt and a couple of dashes of balsamic vinegar, and fry for a further 20 seconds. Pour over half the sherry, add a knob of butter (if using) and half the serrano ham and cook for a further 20 seconds (or longer, if you prefer your liver more cooked). Transfer to an ovenproof dish, cover with foil, place in the oven to keep warm and crack on with the second batch. Just before the second batch is done, return the first batch to the pan and combine everything together. Serve straight away.

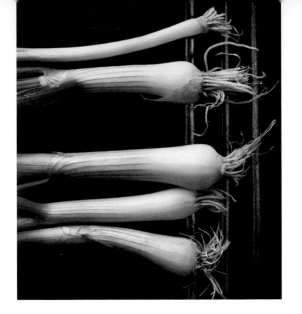

Higadillos con Morcilla

Chicken livers pan-fried with morcilla, spring onions and cream sherry

Chicken livers and morcilla complement each other very well.

Serves 4

400g fresh **chicken livers**, cleaned

2 large **spring onions**, cut into slices 1cm thick

olive oil

Maldon sea salt and **cracked black pepper**, to taste

2 **morcilla sausages** (about 100g in total), preferably Morcilla de Burgos (see page 100), cut into slices 2cm thick

75ml **rich cream sherry**

30g **butter**

Trim away any fat from the livers and remove the sinewy vessel that runs through the middle. Marinate the livers: cut the livers in half and put them and the spring onions in a large bowl with 12 dashes of olive oil and 2 pinches of black pepper. Mix well, cover with clingfilm and leave to marinate in the fridge for 2 hours.

You will have to fry the liver in 2 batches to avoid 'boiling' instead of searing the meat, so have an ovenproof dish ready and preheat your oven to 150ºC/300ºF/gas mark 2.

Place a large, heavy-based, non-stick frying pan on a high heat with 8 dashes of olive oil. When it is smoking hot, drop in half the livers, half the sliced morcilla and a generous pinch of salt, and fry fiercely for 90 seconds, stirring all the time. Pour in half the sherry, add half the butter and cook for a further 40 seconds. Transfer everything to an ovenproof dish, cover with foil, and place in the oven to keep warm while you cook the rest of the livers and morcilla. Just before the second batch is ready, return the first batch to the pan and combine everything together. Serve straight away.

Frito Mallorquin

Chicken livers pan-fried with smoked bacon, potatoes and caramelised red onions

My wife Sarah remembers having this chicken liver dish in Mallorca when she was young. Looking through regional cookery books, the original recipe was with lamb livers and a whole host of other ingredients. We opted for this version.

Serves 4

400g fresh **chicken livers**, cleaned
garlic-infused olive oil (see page 10)
Maldon sea salt and **cracked black pepper**, to taste
2 medium **Desirée potatoes**
2 medium **red onions**, finely sliced
8 slices **smoked back bacon**, cut into fine strips
20g **butter**

Trim away any fat from the livers and remove the sinewy vessel that runs through the middle. Marinate the livers: cut the livers in half and put them in a large bowl with 8 dashes of garlic oil and 2 pinches of black pepper. Mix well, cover with clingfilm and leave to marinate in the fridge for 2 hours.

Meanwhile, peel the potatoes, cut them into largish chunks and place them in a pan of cold water with 2 generous pinches of salt. Bring to the boil, and then simmer until they are still firm but just tender enough to pierce with a knife. Drain, and then leave in the colander to cool.

When you are ready to cook, place a large, heavy-based, non-stick frying pan on a low heat with 12 dashes of garlic oil and 2 pinches of black pepper. When it is hot, drop in the onions and fry gently for 1 minute. Add the strips of bacon and cook together until the onions are soft and tender and the bacon is just beginning to brown. Remove with a slotted spoon and leave in a dish to one side.

Preheat your oven to 150°C/300°F/gas mark 2. Return the frying pan to a medium heat with 5 more dashes of garlic oil and another generous pinch of black pepper. When it is hot, put in the par-boiled potatoes and fry for 6–7 minutes, or until they are golden brown on all sides. They will soak up most of the oil. When they are done, remove them from the pan and place them in the dish with the onions and bacon. Clean the pan, and then put it back on a high heat with 6 more dashes of garlic oil.

When the oil is hot, drop in half of the livers. Season with 2 generous pinches of salt and cook fiercely for 90 seconds. Add half the butter and fry for a further 30 seconds, stirring all the time, to ensure they cook evenly. Transfer the cooked livers to an ovenproof dish, cover with foil, and place in the oven to keep warm while you cook the remaining batch. Shortly after you have added the butter to the second batch, return the first batch of livers to the pan with the onions, bacon and potatoes. Give everything a good stir and let it cook together for 30 seconds. Serve straight away with some lovely bread.

Croquetas de Pollo

Chicken croquettes

Croquettes are always a staple item on any bar menu, or in any household, across Spain. My mum would prepare loads of them, knowing full well that any that were not eaten straight away would be finished off the next day. You can substitute the chicken in this recipe with jamon serrano, chorizo, morcilla, prawns or mixed cooked vegetables.

**Serves 8
(makes 24)**

1 x 1.3–1.5kg **chicken**

1 medium **leek**, washed and roughly chopped

1 large **carrot**, peeled and roughly chopped

1 **bay leaf**

a pinch of whole **black peppercorns**

2 large **Spanish onions**, finely sliced

Maldon sea salt and **cracked black pepper**, to taste

olive oil

50g **butter**

25g **plain flour** for cooking, plus extra for flouring the croquettes

2 **eggs**

1 teacup **breadcrumbs**

sunflower oil, for deep-frying

Place the chicken in a large saucepan, cover it with cold water and put in the leek, carrot, bay leaf and peppercorns. Keep 50g of the onion to one side and add the rest to the pan. Add a pinch of salt and set over a medium heat. Bring to the boil, uncovered, and then turn down the heat to low and simmer gently for 2 hours, or until the meat starts to fall off the bone. Remove the chicken and place it on a plate until cool enough to handle. You will be left with a rich stock for use later. When the chicken has cooled down, pick off as much meat as possible, not forgetting the 'oysters' underneath, and tear into shreds.

Pour 5 dashes of olive oil into a heavy-based non-stick frying pan and place on a low to medium heat. Add the reserved onion slices and fry them for a few seconds, stirring all the time. When they start to sizzle, add the butter, turn down the heat to low and sauté them very gently until the onions are soft and golden brown. Add the shredded chicken and cook for a few minutes, stirring continuously. Now add the flour and 2 pinches of black pepper, and then continue to cook for a further 2 minutes, stirring all the time to coat the chicken.

Meanwhile, taste the chicken stock and adjust the seasoning. Gradually add the stock to the pan, a ladleful at a time, stirring vigorously until you have a thick paste that comes away from the sides of the pan. (If you add too much stock by mistake, dissolve a tablespoon of flour in a cup of cold milk and stir it into the mixture until you see it thickening.) Any leftover stock can be kept in the fridge or freezer to use another time – don't throw it away!

Once you are happy with the consistency of your mixture, spoon it into a flat dish and leave to cool, and then leave to set in the fridge for a minimum of 2 hours (preferably overnight).

You are now ready to mould your croquettes. Break the eggs into a bowl and beat well. Sprinkle the breadcrumbs over a large dinner plate, and place a cupful of flour on another one. Divide the chicken mixture into 24 balls, each the size of a golf ball, or form into ovular shapes (quenelles). Roll each croquette in flour first, and then drop into the beaten egg and finally coat evenly in breadcrumbs. Lay the finished croquettes on a platter, side by side, and leave to set in the fridge for 45 minutes before frying.

When you are ready to cook, preheat your oven to 150°C/300°F/gas mark 2. Pour the sunflower oil into a wide, deep-sided pan to a depth of about 5–6cm on a high heat. When the oil is smoking hot, drop the croquettes, 6 at a time, into the hot oil and cook for 2 minutes, turning them gently, until golden brown all over. Remove with a slotted spoon and drain on kitchen paper, then carefully break one open to check the inside is piping hot. If it is still cold, pop the croquettes back in the hot oil and cook them for 30 seconds longer. When you are satisfied the croquettes are hot, put them in an ovenproof dish, cover with foil, and place in the oven to keep warm while you fry the rest. Serve immediately.

Higadillos de Pato a la Plancha

Chargrilled duck livers

Duck livers are a lot firmer than chicken livers, and they are a lot richer – a bit of an acquired taste, but worth trying. Personally, I prefer them to duck meat. You should be able to buy a fig or berry compote from a good delicatessen or you could always make your own.

Serves 4

400g **fresh duck livers**, cleaned

olive oil

3 **garlic cloves**, thinly sliced

2 sprigs **fresh sage**, coarsely chopped

Maldon sea salt and **cracked black pepper**, to taste

fig or **berry compote**, to serve

Trim away any fat from the livers and remove the sinewy vessel that runs through the middle, but leave them as whole as possible. Marinate the duck livers: place them in a large bowl with 12 dashes of olive oil, the garlic, sage and 3 generous pinches of pepper. Mix well, cover with clingfilm and leave to marinate in the fridge for 2–4 hours.

When you are ready to cook, place your griddle plate on a high heat with 2 dashes of olive oil. When it is smoking hot, place the livers on top, sprinkle 2 pinches of salt over them and chargrill for 50 seconds on each side. Serve with a dollop of fig or berry compote on the side and some toasted bread.

Pato Dulzón

Pan-fried duck with red plums, redcurrants and honey

I am not a great fan of duck – I find the flavour too overpowering and, if not cooked properly, it often ends up as a 'tough old bird'. However, there are plenty of duck lovers among our customers, and this recipe is for you.

Serves 4

3 **duck breasts** (about 200g each), each one cut into 4 strips

garlic-infused olive oil (see page 10)

1 sprig **fresh mint**, finely chopped

Maldon sea salt and **cracked black pepper**, to taste

2 **red plums**, ripe but still firm, cut into quarters

2 tablespoons **redcurrants** (fresh or frozen)

2 teaspoons **clear honey**

balsamic vinegar

First marinate the duck. Place the strips of duck in a large bowl with 7 dashes of garlic oil, the mint, 2 generous pinches of black pepper and salt. Mix well, cover with clingfilm and leave to marinate in the fridge for 2 hours.

When you are ready to cook, preheat your oven to 180°C/350°F/gas mark 4. Place a large, heavy-based, non-stick frying pan on a high heat with 3 dashes of garlic oil (the pan is going into the oven, so make sure it doesn't have a plastic handle). When it is good and hot, carefully lower in the strips of duck, skin-side down, and sear them for a good 30 seconds. Turn them over, season with a generous pinch of salt and cook on the other side for 30 seconds. Now place the pan in the oven to cook for 2 minutes.

Take the pan out of the oven and put it back on a high heat. Drop in the plums and cook until they start to soften. Finally add the redcurrants, honey and balsamic and cook together for a further 20 seconds. Serve straight away.

Pato con Membrillo

Pan-fried duck with quince, butter beans and spring onions

A sweet/savoury combination of flavours always complements the strong flavour of duck meat. Pear is a classic choice, so we decided to add quince with its slightly tart undertones. The butter beans was a surprise addition by the chefs to give the dish some substance but their creaminess really goes well with everything else.

Serves 4

3 **duck breasts** (about 200g each), each one cut into 4 strips

garlic-infused olive oil (see page 10)

1 sprig **fresh mint**, finely chopped

Maldon sea salt and **cracked black pepper**, to taste

25g **butter**

2 **spring onions**, finely sliced

1 x 400g tin (or jar) **butter beans** in water

2 tablespoons quince jelly (most good delicatessens will have some good quince jam or jelly – membrillo)

First marinate the duck as in the recipe on page 90.

Preheat your oven to 180°C/350°F/gas mark 4. When you are ready to cook, place a large, heavy-based, non-stick frying pan on a low heat with 7 dashes of garlic oil (the pan's going to go in the oven, so make sure it doesn't have a plastic handle). When it is hot, add 10g of the butter and the spring onions. Fry gently, stirring regularly, until the onions are soft and golden. Remove them with a slotted spoon and place in a dish on one side.

Turn up the heat to medium and drop in the strips of duck, skin-side down. Fry for 30 seconds on the first side, and then turn them over with a spatula and season with a generous pinch of salt. Cook for 60 seconds on the other side, and then place the pan in the oven to cook for 2 minutes.

Meanwhile, drain the butter beans. When the 2 minutes are up, use an oven glove and take the pan out of the oven and put it back on a medium heat. Add the spring onions, membrillo, butter beans and the remaining butter, and cook together for a further 20 seconds, stirring all the time. Serve straight away.

Panceta Asada

Slow roast belly of pork marinated with fennel seeds and garlic

Certain cuts of pork can be quite dry, especially if they have no layer of fat to draw juices from during the cooking process. This is not the case, however, with belly of pork. My grandmother would use belly of pork to flavour her stews, and it always braised beautifully. When she took it out, she would eat the meat and spread the soft layer of fat on slices of bread. Even when she roasted it slowly in the oven, the layer of fat and any meat that came off would be soft enough to spread on bread or mash into boiled potatoes. Cob, amongst other things, slow roasts pork beautifully.

Serves 8

3kg **belly of pork**, unsmoked and boned

olive oil

7 **garlic cloves**, thinly sliced

2 tablespoons **fennel seeds**, crushed

1 cupful **Maldon sea salt**

Place the pork, skin-side up, on a chopping board. Using the tip of a sharp knife, score the skin on the diagonal with slashes about 1cm apart, then repeat in the opposite direction to give a cross-hatching pattern. Turn the meat over and puncture the flesh all over with a skewer, making sure you don't go all the way through.

In a small bowl, combine 7 dashes of olive oil with the sliced garlic and crushed fennel seeds. Using a tablespoon, drizzle the mixture over the underside of the pork (not the skin) and rub it in well with your fingers.

Turn the meat over and rub as much salt as possible into the skin. Then wrap the whole thing in clingfilm and leave to marinate in the fridge for 24 hours.

When you are ready to cook, preheat your oven to 230ºC/450ºF/gas mark 8. Remove the pork from the fridge, take off the clingfilm, then place skin-side up on a wire rack over a roasting tin. Place in the oven on the top shelf for 30 minutes to sear the skin. Then reduce the heat to 190ºC/375ºF/gas mark 5 and cook for a further 2^1/$_2$ hours. If you like your skin really crisp, put the pork under the grill for a few minutes before serving until you have the desired effect. When done, place on a chopping board and leave to rest for 7 minutes. Slice into portions and serve.

Salteado de Col con Panceta

Pan-fried savoy cabbage with smoked bacon, caramelised onions
and paprika

The combination of pork and cabbage crosses many culinary borders. This recipe also works well with Rosario chorizo or morcilla.

Serves 6

olive oil

1/2 teaspoon smoked **sweet paprika**

1 **Savoy cabbage**

Maldon sea salt and **cracked black pepper**, to taste

25g **unsalted butter**

2 medium **onions**, finely chopped

8 rashers **smoked back bacon**, coarsely chopped

Pour 3 dashes of olive oil into a cup and add the paprika. Stir vigorously until blended, then leave to one side to infuse.

Pull the leaves off the cabbage, keeping as many of the outer, dark green leaves as possible. Discard any that are too far gone, along with the core. Coarsely tear the leaves you have selected, wash them thoroughly and put them in a pan of boiling water with a generous pinch of salt. Cook until the cabbage is tender but still with a bit of bite – this should take 1–1¹/₂ minutes, but check it regularly. Drain and put to one side.

Place a large, heavy-based, non-stick frying pan (or wok) on a low to medium heat with 7 dashes of olive oil. When it is smoking hot, add the butter, onion, 1 pinch of salt and pepper and then fry, stirring regularly, until the onion is golden brown. Remove them with a slotted spoon and place them in a dish to one side. Return the pan to a medium heat and gently fry the bacon until it just starts to brown. Remove with a slotted spoon and place with the onions.

If your pan (or wok) is big enough to hold the cabbage and the other ingredients use that. If not, place a large roasting tray on the hob instead. Heat the paprika oil over a medium to high heat, and then add the cabbage. Cook for 2 minutes, stirring all the time, to allow the flavoured oil to infuse the cabbage. Add the onions, bacon and 2 pinches of pepper and cook for a further 3 minutes, or until everything is good and hot. Serve immediately.

Solomillo de Cerdo a la Plancha

Pork loin marinated in garlic, coriander and harissa

If you wish, you can add some chopped dates or prunes to the pork when you marinate it, and put them on the griddle as well.

Serves 4

600g **pork tenderloin** (roughly 2 whole ones)

olive oil

1/2 teaspoon **harissa paste**

3 **garlic cloves**, thinly sliced

Maldon sea salt and **cracked black pepper**, to taste

3 sprigs **fresh coriander**, coarsely chopped

1 large, firm **beef tomato**

4 **lime** wedges, to serve

First prepare the marinade for the pork. Pour 125ml of olive oil into a measuring jug and stir in the harissa, garlic, 1 generous pinch of pepper and the fresh coriander. Beat well.

Cut the tenderloins (which are long tube-like strips of meat) in half, then in half again to give you 8 chunky slices of pork. Stretch a piece of clingfilm over your chopping board and lay two pieces of pork on top (so the flat sides are facing up and down). Cover them with another piece of clingfilm, and then bash them flat with a meat mallet (or rolling pin) until they are about 9cm in diameter – be careful not to tear them. Repeat with the remaining pieces of pork, and then place them in a large bowl. Pour over the marinade and dig in with your hands to coat the meat thoroughly. Cover the bowl with clingfilm and leave to marinate in the fridge for 12 hours.

Set your griddle plate on a high heat with 6 dashes of olive oil to get smoking hot. Meanwhile, cut the tomato into four slices and sprinkle each one with a pinch of salt and pepper. When the griddle is hot, put the tomato slices on top and cook for 1 minute on each side. Transfer them to an ovenproof dish, cover with foil, and place in the oven to keep warm.

Scrape the tomato residue off the griddle with a spatula and add 2 more dashes of oil. Lay the flattened pieces of pork on the griddle and sprinkle with a pinch of salt. Sear them for 40 seconds on each side. Serve on a large platter with a tomato slice between each slice of pork, and lime wedges on the side.

Patatas con Jamón Serrano, Ajo y Tomatitos

Sautéed potatoes with serrano ham, garlic and roasted cherry tomatoes

When my mother had nothing in the fridge to cook, she would turn to the store-cupboard. Invariably, she would keep certain stock items – potatoes, garlic, olive oil, tins of pulses and salted meats. In Spain, there is a recipe called 'patatas a lo pobre' – 'poor man's potatoes'. It's basically a potato recipe with any leftovers thrown in. And that is what my mother would cook. Using a sharp knife, she would cut off some very, very thin slivers of meat from a piece of salted pork and rub off any excess salt, then cut them into thin strips and fry them with some boiled potatoes and garlic, and anything else she could lay her hands on. Every dish would taste different, but they would always be delicious. Here we have substituted the salted pork for serrano ham, and added some roasted cherry tomatoes for colour.

Serves 4

5 medium **Desirée red potatoes,** peeled and cut into slices 2cm thick

olive oil

8 thin slices **jamon serrano**

2 large **garlic cloves**, thinly sliced

2 sprigs **fresh thyme**

12 **cherry tomatoes**, roasted in olive oil and salt at 150°C/300°F/gas mark 2 for 1 hour, or until soft

Maldon sea salt and **cracked black pepper**, to taste

Place the potatoes in a large pan of cold salted water. Bring to the boil, then cook until they are just tender enough to pierce them with a knife. Drain and leave to one side.

Place a large, heavy-based, non-stick frying pan on a low heat with 6 dashes of olive oil. When the pan is hot, lay the slices of serrano ham flat inside and let them fry very gently for 2–3 minutes. The idea is to let them release some of their flavour. When they start to crisp, remove them from the pan and slice them into thin strips. Place in a dish to one side.

Return the pan to a low heat with 12 more dashes of olive oil. This might sound like a lot, but the potatoes will absorb much of it. When the oil is hot, add the garlic and fry gently until it starts to colour. Drop in the thyme and continue to cook very gently until the garlic is golden and the thyme starts to change colour. Remove with a slotted spoon and put with the ham.

If your pan is big enough to hold the potatoes, use that. If not, place a large roasting tray on the hob and pour the thyme- and garlic-infused oil from the frying pan into that. Turn up the heat to medium, and then add the par-boiled potatoes and 2 generous pinches of pepper and 1 of salt. Fry the potatoes until they just start to brown, then add the garlic, serrano ham and tomatoes. Carry on cooking for 2 minutes, or until the ingredients have married together nicely. Serve immediately.

Albóndigas en Salsa de Tomate

Pork meatballs in a rich tomato sauce

Meatballs. Now here's another dish that conjures up childhood memories. Watching my mum prepare the 'sofrito' – rolling the balls... making the sauce... eating them and then mopping up the juices with bread... and feeling warm. Meatballs are universal – Polish, Swedish, Jewish or Italian – every country has its own recipe. I'm sure most of us can recall a family recipe handed down from somewhere up the family tree.

We use pork for our meatballs because we find it more flavoursome and juicier than beef, and we cook them in a rich tomato sauce. The man responsible for making them at El Parador is our commis chef, August, another long-standing staff member and one of the loveliest human beings I have ever encountered. I don't think he has a single drop of bad blood in his body, always positive and there to do his best. And this karma passes through to his cooking. Not only does he make a cracking Alioli and Romanesco, not to mention the cheese and spinach mix for the Empanadillas (see page 133), but he's also got the meatball recipe down to a tee. Even my mum approved of it, and she passed it on to him!

Serves 8
(makes 24)

650g lean, **minced pork**

2 pinches each of finely chopped **fresh rosemary**, **thyme**, **mint**, **basil**, **tarragon**, **coriander** and **oregano** – yes, there are a lot of herbs, but they do add to the flavour (try to resist using plain, dried mixed herbs, unless that's all you have)

1 **egg**

$1/2$ **Spanish onion**, finely diced

2 **garlic cloves**, finely chopped

$1/2$ **red chilli**, deseeded and finely chopped

300g **fresh breadcrumbs**

Maldon sea salt and **cracked black pepper**, to taste

olive oil

for the rich tomato sauce

olive oil

$1/2$ **Spanish onion**, finely chopped

1 medium **carrot**, peeled and finely diced

1 stick **celery**, finely diced

Maldon sea salt and **cracked black pepper**, to taste

70ml **ruby port** (or Oloroso sherry)

250ml **red wine**

3 x 400g tins chopped **plum tomatoes**

10 **fresh basil leaves**, coarsely torn

2 **bay leaves**

Preheat your oven to 180°C/350°F/gas mark 4. Start with the meatballs. In a large bowl, combine the minced pork, herbs, egg, onion, garlic, chilli, breadcrumbs and 3 generous pinches of salt and pepper. Dig in with your hands and combine well. Oil your hands and then start forming the meatballs. You should end up with around 24 reasonably sized meatballs (although obviously you can make them smaller, if you wish).

Pour 15 dashes of olive oil into a large roasting tray to heat up on the top of the stove. Drop in the meatballs, stirring them around to coat them evenly in the oil. Place the tray in the oven for 30 minutes, or until the meatballs are golden brown all over – you will need to keep an eye on them and stir them occasionally to make sure they are browning evenly.

Meanwhile, crack on with the tomato sauce. Place a large, deep-sided saucepan on a low heat and pour in 8 dashes of olive oil. Add the finely chopped onion, carrot and celery and a couple of pinches of salt and pepper. Fry gently together until the vegetables soften and just start to colour. Pour in the port (or sherry) and red wine and bring to the boil. Add the tomatoes, basil, bay leaves and a couple more pinches of salt and pepper and bring back to the boil, stirring all the time. Turn down the heat to low and simmer gently for 15 minutes.

Once the meatballs are brown, spoon them carefully into the cooked tomato sauce and allow them to cook together for a further 10 minutes. Serve with fresh, crusty bread.

Morcilla de Burgos Salteado con Judías Verdes, Champiñones y Queso Feta

Morcilla pan-fried with green beans, chestnut mushrooms and feta cheese

Morcilla is the Spanish version of black pudding. It is flavoured with various ingredients, depending on the region – including rice, pork fat, pinenuts, almonds, cinnamon, mint or cloves. Our favourite one, from Burgos in northern Spain, has a high rice content and not so much obvious fat (although it is there).

Serves 4

olive oil

2 large **garlic cloves**, thinly sliced

4 **morcilla sausages** (about 200g in total), preferably Morcilla de Burgos, cut into rounds 1cm thick

12 **chestnut mushrooms**, cut in half

Maldon sea salt and **cracked black pepper**, to taste

20 **fine green beans**, blanched in boiling water until just tender

75g **feta cheese**, cut into cubes the size of sugar lumps

Heat 4 dashes of olive oil in a large, heavy-based frying pan (or wok) on a medium heat. Add the sliced garlic and let it brown, stirring and ensuring it does not burn, then drop in the slices of morcilla. Fry for a minute or so, or until browned on both sides – don't worry if the slices break up a bit – and then remove with a slotted spoon and leave to one side. Bear in mind you may have to fry the sausgaes in two batches.

Return the pan to a medium heat with 4 more dashes of oil. Drop in the halved mushrooms and season with salt and pepper. Stir-fry for 3–4 minutes, or until the mushrooms have softened, and then add 6 dashes of olive oil, the browned morcilla and garlic, and the blanched green beans. Stir everything together so it heats through evenly – the morcilla will probably break up even more (if you want to avoid this then add the morcilla right at the end, so keep it in a preheated oven at 150°C/300°F/gas mark 2 and then place on the top of the other ingredients when serving). Drop in the cubes of feta cheese. Keep on turning the ingredients in the pan until the feta starts to melt, then spoon onto serving plates and serve immediately.

Morcilla con Patatas Estrelladas

Grilled morcilla with crushed new potatoes, garlic and spring onions

The following recipe is our version of a 'Spanish fry-up'. If you want to finish it off just add an egg fried with padron peppers (see page 137).

Serves 4

14 small **new potatoes**

Maldon sea salt and **cracked black pepper**, to taste

50g **butter**

olive oil

4 **morcilla sausages** (about 200g in total), preferably Morcilla de Burgos, cut into slices 1cm thick

2 large **garlic cloves**, thinly sliced

2 large **spring onions**, cleaned and thinly sliced

Place the potatoes in a large pan of cold water with 3 pinches of salt. Bring to the boil, then cook until they are just tender enough to pierce with a knife. Drain and put them back in the pan with the butter and 3 generous pinches of pepper. Using a potato masher, gently crush the potatoes to burst them, and then cover the pan with a lid and leave to one side.

Put your griddle plate on a high heat with 4 dashes of olive oil. When it is smoking hot, drop in the slices of morcilla and brown them on both sides.

Meanwhile, place a small frying pan on a low heat with 15 dashes of olive oil. When it is hot, drop in the garlic, the spring onions and a pinch of salt, and fry gently until soft and golden.

To serve, place a dollop of the crushed potato on each plate, arrange 4 slices of morcilla on top and spoon over some of the garlic and spring onions.

Morcilla con Pimientos y Habas Verdes

Grilled morcilla with chargrilled red peppers, broad beans and red onions

'Spanish fry-up part 2'. A savoury heaven. We love chargrilled or roasted red peppers. The slight sweetness of the red onions just infuses the dish enough. The broad beans are a welcome change from baked beans!

Serves 4

2 medium **red peppers**

garlic-infused olive oil (see page 10)

Maldon sea salt and **cracked black pepper**, to taste

2 small **red onions**, finely sliced

4 **morcilla sausages** (about 200g in total), preferably Morcilla de Burgos, cut into slices 2cm thick

1 handful **frozen broad beans** (husks removed), defrosted if frozen

Spike the peppers with skewers and hold them over a high flame on the stove until the skins are charred and black – wear oven gloves for this because the skewers will get hot. Leave the peppers to cool down slightly, and then peel off the skins. It helps if you wrap the peppers in clingfilm first. Place your griddle, ridged-side up, on a high heat. Cut off the tops from the peppers, remove the seeds and chargrill the flesh on the hot griddle. Leave to cool, and then cut into thin strips and leave in a dish to one side. Clean the griddle plate and leave it on a low heat.

Place a large, heavy-based, non-stick frying pan on a low heat with 10 dashes of garlic oil, 2 pinches of black pepper and 1 of salt. When the oil is hot, add the onions and fry them gently until soft and tender. Add the sliced peppers and give them a good stir.

Meanwhile, increase the heat under the griddle to medium and fry the slices of morcilla until brown on both sides.

Add the broad beans and morcilla to the peppers and onions and cook together for 1 minute, stirring carefully, or until the beans have heated through.

Chori-pan

Braised spicy Rosario chorizo and onion hot dogs

The next dish is not on the menu that often but is very popular when it is.

Serves 8

olive oil

2 large **white onions**, thinly sliced

Maldon sea salt and **cracked black pepper**, to taste

8 spicy **Rosario chorizo sausages**

500ml **red wine**

1 **bay leaf**

8 **hot dog rolls**

Place a large casserole dish on a low heat, add 12 dashes of olive oil, the onions, 2 pinches of pepper and 1 of salt and fry until the onions are soft and golden. Remove them with a slotted spoon and leave to one side.

Return the casserole (with the oil) to a low heat, add in the sausages (whole) and cook them until their skins start to colour. Return the cooked onions to the casserole and give everything a good stir. Pour over enough wine to cover the sausages and onions, if necessary topping up with water. Add the bay leaf and another pinch of salt, and then turn up the heat and bring to the boil. Now turn down the heat, cover and simmer gently for 50 minutes, stirring occasionally.

When the sausages are done, cut open the rolls. To serve, slot a sausage and a good measure of onions into each roll and enjoy.

NB: If you can wait until the next day, the flavour of the sausages really improves after 24 hours in the fridge. Just make sure you bring everything to the boil again and then simmer for 20 minutes before serving.

Rosario Chorizo con Pimientos Asados y Fundador

Rosario chorizo pan-fried with roasted peppers and Fundador brandy

Chorizo sausage is the most popular sausage throughout Spain. It comes in different shapes and sizes, hot or mild in seasoning, smoked or unsmoked, according to its regional background. The meat used is generally pork, although venison can be found in the Pyrenean region of Spain. Flavouring ingredients include garlic, smoked or unsmoked paprika, herbs or chilli. Chorizo used in cooking usually has a higher fat content, while ones reserved for slicing and eating are air-cured and denser in texture. You can substitute the brandy for some Anis Seco (an aniseed-based drink) – make sure it's the dry version, not the sweet one.

Serves 4

2 medium **red peppers**

olive oil

Maldon sea salt, to taste

garlic-infused olive oil (see page 10)

8 spicy **Rosario chorizo sausages**, cut into slices 2cm thick

50ml **Fundador brandy**

2 sprigs **flat-leaf parsley**, coarsely chopped

Spike the 2 peppers with skewers and hold them over a high flame on the stove until the skin is charred and black – wear oven gloves for this because the skewers will get hot. Leave the peppers to cool down slightly, then peel off the skins and hull them.

Place 2 dashes of olive oil in a heavy-based frying pan and put on a medium heat. Add the skinned peppers and sear them quickly all over. Remove them from the pan and place in a dish. Sprinkle over a couple of pinches of salt and 2 dashes of garlic oil, allow them to cool, and then cover the dish with clingfilm and leave to marinate in the fridge for 2 hours. Once done, cut the peppers into thin slices and leave to one side.

Preheat your oven to 150°C/300°F/gas mark 2. Place a clean, large, heavy-based frying pan (or wok) on a high heat. Add 2 dashes of olive oil and tilt the pan backwards and forwards to coat the base completely. When the oil is smoking hot, drop in half the sausages and cook them fiercely until they start to brown and release their fat. At this point, put in half the sliced, marinated peppers and cook for 20 seconds more. If you are cooking on gas, be careful: the fat will spit and may ignite – it looks fancy, just don't burn your house down! The pan will ignite when you pour in half the brandy. Pour it in now and cook for another 10 seconds, then toss in half the parsley. Transfer to an ovenproof dish and place in the oven to keep warm while you fry the second batch in the same way. When the second batch is almost ready, return the first batch to the pan and give everything a good stir. Serve straight away.

Rosario con Patatas

Spicy Rosario chorizo pan-fried with sautéed potatoes

The par-boiled potatoes in this dish soak up the juices from the sausages and the garlic infused oil – another dish worthy of a fried egg on top.

Serves 4

2 medium **Desirée red potatoes**
garlic-infused oil (see page 10)
8 spicy **Rosario chorizo sausages**, cut into slices 1.5cm thick
Maldon sea salt and **cracked black pepper**, to taste

Peel the potatoes, cut them in half, and then cut each half into slices 1.5cm thick. Place in a pan of cold, salted water and bring to the boil. Parboil, or until just tender enough to pierce with a knife. Drain and leave to one side.

Preheat your oven to 150°C/300°F/gas mark 2. Place a heavy-based frying pan on a high heat and pour in 3 dashes of garlic oil, and tilt the pan backwards and forwards to coat the base completely. When it is good and hot, toss in half the chorizo slices and fry for 20 seconds, stirring, until the chorizo starts to brown on both sides and begins to release its fat. If you're cooking on gas, be careful: the fat from the sausages will start to spit and could ignite. Add half the potatoes, a generous pinch of pepper and a pinch of salt, and continue to cook for a further 30 seconds. The potatoes will take on the reddish colour of the chorizo as they absorb the juices from the sausages. Once done, spoon into an ovenproof dish and place in the oven to keep warm while you fry the second batch. Just before the second batch is ready, add the first batch back to the pan and give everything a good stir. Serve straight away.

Salteado de Cordero Adobado

Strips of lamb marinated with cumin and coriander, pan-fried with roasted cherry tomatoes

The North African spices combine beautifully with lamb. The juices from the cherry tomatoes blend with those of the lamb to give a delicious sauce that beckons you to dunk some bread into it.

Serves 4-6

600g **leg of lamb**, boned, trimmed and cut into strips the length of your thumb and twice as thick

olive oil

1 teaspoon **cumin powder**

3 sprigs **fresh coriander**, coarsely chopped

Maldon sea salt and **cracked black pepper**, to taste

12 **cherry tomatoes**, roasted in olive oil and salt at 150°C/300°F/gas mark 2 for 1 hour, or until soft

First marinate the meat. Put the lamb strips in a large bowl with 120ml olive oil, the cumin, fresh coriander and 2 generous pinches of pepper. Combine well, and then cover with clingfilm and leave to marinate in the fridge for 12 hours.

When you are ready to cook, preheat your oven to 150°C/300°F/gas mark 2.

Place a large, heavy-based, non-stick frying pan on a high heat with 6 dashes of olive oil. When it is smoking hot, put in half the strips of lamb and 1 generous pinch of salt and cook them for 1 minute on each side. Add in half the tomatoes, another pinch of salt and cook for a further 1 minute. Transfer the lamb and tomatoes to an ovenproof dish, cover with foil, place in the oven to keep warm while you cook the second batch. Just before the second batch is ready, return the first batch to the pan and give everything a good stir and cook for 1 minute more. Serve straight away.

Cordero a la Plancha

Grilled lamb marinated with rosemary, garlic and olive oil served with spicy zhoug

We either grill or pan-fry lamb. Either way we always marinate it to tenderise and enhance its flavour. We tend to use a leg of lamb that has been boned and trimmed of any excess fat. A good butcher will bone the meat for you. Zhoug is a spicy marinade from Yemen. It packs a mighty, refreshing punch and can be used to accompany many other meats. I find it too powerful to go with fish, but try it out by all means. It can be kept in the fridge, covered with a layer of olive oil, for 3–5 days.

Serves 8

1kg **leg of lamb**, boned and trimmed

2 large **garlic cloves**, finely sliced

3 sprigs **fresh rosemary**

olive oil

Maldon sea salt and **cracked black pepper**, to taste

for the zhoug (makes 1kg tub)

1 tablespoon **cardamom seeds**, de-husked

1¹/₂ tablespoons **coriander seeds**

1¹/₂ tablespoons **cumin seeds**

75ml **olive oil**

1kg **green chillies** (seeds removed)

4 **garlic cloves**

juice of ³/₄ **lemon**

Maldon sea salt

First marinate the meat. Cut the lamb into 16 slices – try to cut it along the grain of the muscle, as this will allow the meat to relax and makes it more tender. Place the slices in a large bowl and add the garlic, rosemary, 10 dashes of olive oil and 2 pinches of pepper. Mix in well to coat the meat, then cover with clingfilm and leave to marinate in the fridge for 2 hours minimum (12 hours maximum, if possible).

Now prepare the zhoug. Place a small, heavy-based frying pan on a low heat. Do not add any oil. When it is hot, put in the cardamom, coriander and cumin seeds and fry gently until lightly toasted – do not let them burn! Pour the olive oil into a food-processor and add the roasted seeds, chillies, garlic, lemon juice and 2 generous pinches of salt. Blend to a smooth, thick paste.

When you're ready to cook the lamb, place your griddle plate on a high heat. Do not add oil. When it starts to smoke, put on the slices of lamb (along with the rosemary and garlic from the marinade), sprinkle with a pinch of salt and cook for 30 seconds on each side. Serve with a dollop of zhoug on the side.

vegetables

I have known chefs who have turned their noses up at cooking vegetarian food – not vegetables, but food for vegetarians. To this day, not one of them has justified their reaction. You can get a cornucopia of vegetables in Spain (and all of the Mediterranean), but how many times have you gone into a local Spanish/French/Italian restaurant abroad and not found anything that is strictly vegetarian? Waiting staff often explain in a bewildered fashion when proffering a supposedly vegetarian option: 'Solo tiene un poquito de jamón serrano para darle sabor...' ('It's only got a bit of serrano ham in it to give it flavour...'). At El Parador we like our vegetarian food... especially Juliet... and we like variety.

Tortilla Española

Potato and caramelised onion omelette

Ubiquitous throughout Spain, the tortilla can be served as a starter, main course, sandwich filling, tapa or canapé, either hot or cold. We serve it at room temperature, or just above, and cook it so it's still slightly moist in the centre. Our one is good, but I have to doff my hat to the one served at Moro in Exmouth Market, London. As well as the many beautiful dishes they serve (and they serve plenty of them), the simple, classic tortilla is consistently good and by far the best I've tasted in London. This is our version.

Serves 8

1.5kg **Desirée red potatoes**
olive oil
1 large **Spanish onion**, thinly sliced
Maldon sea salt and **cracked black pepper**, to taste
knob of **butter**
10 **eggs**

Peel the potatoes, cut them in half, and then cut each half into slices 1.5cm thick. Place in a pan of cold, salted water and bring to the boil. Parboil, or until just tender enough to pierce with a knife. Drain and leave to one side.

In a large, non-stick frying pan, around 30cm in diameter (preferably with sloping sides because it will make turning the tortilla easier later on), pour in 12 dashes of olive oil and put on a low to medium heat. Toss in the sliced onions and a generous pinch of salt and pepper, and start to fry them. Once the onions start to sizzle, turn the heat down to low and add the knob of butter. Cook the onions until they are soft and golden, and then remove them with a slotted spoon and leave to one side.

Return the pan to a medium heat, add the par-boiled potatoes, a generous pinch of salt and a small pinch of pepper and fry gently for about 2 minutes, turning frequently, or until the potatoes are lightly crisp and golden on the outside and soft on the inside. Just before they are done, return the cooked onions to the pan, stir them in well and cook together for about a minute. When done, remove everything with a slotted spoon and place in a bowl to one side. You'll need the oil that's left in the pan for later.

Crack the eggs into a large bowl, add 2 generous pinches of salt and beat lightly together. Add the cooked potato and onion mixture and stir well. Leave to stand for a few minutes to allow the ingredients to marry.

Return the pan to a medium to high heat, add 6 more dashes of olive oil and tilt the pan backwards and forwards to coat the bottom. Heat the oil until smoking hot, then pour in the egg mixture, moving the pan in a gentle, circular motion to distribute the ingredients evenly and prevent the egg from sticking and burning. Cook for about 30 seconds, then turn down the heat to medium-low and cook for a further 4 minutes, shaking the pan gently every so often. Do not stir! When the tortilla starts to bubble at the sides, it's time to turn it over. If this is your first time at doing this, be prepared for some mess and be careful not to get burnt.

Find a suitable plate large enough to cover the face of the pan with space to spare and set it face-down on top. Hold firmly onto the handle of the pan with one hand, and use the other hand to press down firmly on the plate. Now in one fast move, lift the pan off the stove and flip it over onto the plate. Remove the pan (hopefully there'll be little, if anything, left stuck to the base) and place it back on a high heat. Set down the plate while you heat up 5 more dashes of olive oil in the pan. When the oil is smoking hot, carefully slide the half-cooked tortilla back into the pan to cook on the other side. You might need to shake the pan gently and tuck in the sides of the tortilla with a wooden spatula because they'll probably be looking a bit jagged. Allow the tortilla to cook on a high heat for 30 seconds, then reduce the heat to medium and cook for a further 4 minutes. This should leave you with a tortilla that's moist in the middle – if you prefer it firmer, cook for a minute or so longer.

When the tortilla is cooked to your liking, slide it onto a clean plate to cool down slightly. Serve hot, warm or at room temperature, either sliced into 8 hearty wedges, or cut into small cubes to serve as little canapés.

Tortilla con Espinacas y Queso de Cabra

Spinach and goat's cheese tortilla

Once you have mastered how to make a tortilla, you can add other ingredients to the basic mixture.

Serves 8

1kg **Desirée red potatoes**
1 large **Spanish onion**, thinly sliced
olive oil
knob of **butter**
500g fresh, **young leaf spinach**, washed
Maldon sea salt and **cracked black pepper**, to taste
10 **eggs**
75g **soft goat's cheese**

Prepare and cook the potatoes and onions in olive oil and butter, according to the recipe for Tortilla Espanola on page 112.

Meanwhile, place a large, heavy-based frying pan on a high heat with 2 dashes of olive oil. When the oil is smoking hot, put in the spinach, add a pinch of salt and turn the leaves gently in the pan until they start to wilt. Just as the spinach starts to release its water, remove the pan from the heat and tip the spinach into a bowl lined with kitchen paper to soak up the bitter cooking juices.

Crack the eggs into a large bowl, add 2 generous pinches of salt and beat lightly together. Add the cooked potatoes, onions and spinach, and crumble in the goat's cheese. Leave to stand for a few minutes, and then cook the tortilla according to the instructions on page 113.

Puré de Berenjenas Asadas con Patatas

Roasted aubergine and potato mash cakes

Roasted aubergine is delicious. Roasted aubergine and potato mash cakes with lots of black pepper, some extra virgin olive oil and a bit of butter are divine.

Serves 4

2 large **Desirée red potatoes**, peeled and roughly chopped
Maldon sea salt and **cracked black pepper**, to taste
50g **butter**
2 large **aubergines**, cut in half lengthways
extra virgin olive oil
3 **garlic cloves**, finely sliced

Preheat your oven to 200°C/400°F/gas mark 6. Place the potatoes in a pan of cold water with 3 generous pinches of salt and bring to the boil. Cook until the potatoes are soft, and then drain thoroughly and return to the pan. Drop in the butter and 3 generous pinches of pepper and cover with a lid.

Meanwhile, place the aubergines in a roasting tray, baste with a little olive oil and roast them in the oven for 15 minutes, or until the flesh is soft and brown. Remove from the oven and scoop out the flesh. Discard the skins and add the flesh to the potatoes.

Place a small frying pan on a low heat with 10 dashes of extra virgin olive oil. Add the garlic and fry gently until soft and golden. When it is done, put it in the pan with the potatoes and aubergines, along with the garlic oil, and mash everything together to a coarse paste. Season to taste.

Place a large griddle plate on a high heat with 3 dashes of olive oil. When it is smoking hot, form the potato and aubergine mash into patties the size of a beefburger and pop them on the griddle. Grill until crisp and golden brown on both sides.

Patatas Bravas

Spicy sautéed potatoes in a rich tomato sauce

Another dish that is closely associated with Spain is 'Patatas Bravas'. I have had so many variations of them throughout Spain from the ridiculous – chips splattered with tomato ketchup, not even Heinz, mixed with Worcestershire Sauce – to the sublime, beautifully cooked potatoes, slightly crunchy, good and spicy on the outside, soft in the middle, all coated in a lovely rich tomato sauce.

Serves 8

8 large **Desirée red potatoes**, unpeeled

1¹/₂ teaspoons **chilli powder**

1¹/₂ teaspoons **hot smoked paprika**

Maldon sea salt and **cracked black pepper**, to taste

1 quantity **rich tomato sauce** (see page 99)

Preheat your oven to 240°C/475°F/gas mark 9.

Cut each potato in half, and then cut into 2.5cm chunks. Place the potatoes in a roasting tray and sprinkle over the chilli powder, paprika, 4 generous pinches of pepper and 2 pinches of salt. Place the tray in the oven and roast for 20 minutes.

While the potatoes are roasting, prepare the rich tomato sauce (see page 99).

When the potatoes are done, take the tray out of the oven and place on top of the hob. Ladle in as much, or as little, of the sauce as you wish and combine well. Serve straight away in individual dishes.

Papas Estrelladas con Romero

Crushed new potatoes with rosemary, garlic and chilli oil

This potato dish is great as an accompaniment to any meat or fish, but it is also lovely on its own.

Serves 4

chilli-infused olive oil (see page 10)

3 **garlic cloves**, finely sliced

3 sprigs **fresh rosemary**

15 medium **new potatoes,** halved and boiled until tender with 2 generous pinches of salt, and drained

Maldon sea salt and **cracked black pepper**, to taste

30g **butter** (optional)

Place a heavy-based frying pan on a low to medium heat and pour in 10 dashes of chilli oil. When the oil is hot, add the slices of garlic and cook gently, stirring all the time, until the garlic just starts to change colour. Remove the leaves from 2 of the sprigs of rosemary and add them to the pan. Continue to cook for 2–3 minutes, or until the garlic is golden brown and the rosemary fades in colour. Remove the garlic and rosemary with a slotted spoon and set aside. Keep the oil in the pan, off the heat.

When the potatoes are cooked, place the frying pan back on a low flame to heat up again. When the oil is hot, pour it over the drained potatoes, and then add the leaves from the remaining sprig of rosemary, a generous pinch of black pepper and the fried garlic and rosemary. For those of you who love your butter, this is the time to add it. Get your potato masher and start to 'burst' – not mash – the potatoes. Then, with a wooden spoon, beat well to incorporate everything together. To serve, drizzle a little more chilli oil over the top.

Pure de Papas del Olivo

Garlic mash with extra virgin olive oil

A potato recipe for garlic and olive oil fiends.

Serves 4

extra virgin olive oil

4 large **Desirée potatoes**, peeled, halved and boiled until tender with 2 generous pinches of salt, and drained

4 whole **garlic cloves,** use garlic confit (see page 10)

Maldon sea salt and **cracked black pepper**, to taste

Add 4 dashes of extra virgin olive oil to the drained potatoes, drop in the whole garlic cloves and season with 2 generous pinches of salt and pepper and mash. The oil will dilute the mash. If it is still solid, add a further 2 dashes of oil if you want a strong olive oil flavour. Serve straight away with a drizzle of oil over each portion.

Puré de Batatas con Queso de Cabra y Puerros

Sweet potato cakes with goat's cheese, leeks and butter

This recipe was one of Juliet's suggestions.

**Serves 4
(makes 8)**

6 large **sweet potatoes**, peeled and cut into chunks

Maldon sea salt and **cracked black pepper**, to taste

60g **butter**

100g **soft goat's cheese**

olive oil

1 medium **leek**, washed and thinly sliced

Put the sweet potatoes in a large saucepan of salted water and boil until soft. Drain, then mash with half the butter and the goat's cheese. The texture doesn't have to be too smooth, so don't worry if it looks a bit lumpy.

Place a heavy-based frying pan on a low heat with 10 dashes of olive oil. When the oil is hot, add the rest of the butter, the sliced leeks and a pinch of salt and pepper. Sauté the leeks gently, stirring occasionally, until they start to turn a lovely golden brown colour. Remove from the heat and leave to cool slightly before adding to the mash. Mix well.

Place your griddle plate on a medium to high heat. Meanwhile, divide the potato mixture into 8 equal portions and shape into patties roughly the size of beefburgers. When the griddle is smoking hot, cook the potato cakes until golden brown on both sides. Serve straight away with a drizzle of olive oil over the top.

Salteado de Batatas

Roasted sweet potatoes pan-fried with roasted red onions,
pinenuts and feta cheese

Lovely ingredients, strong flavours and delicious textures make this a very
popular dish at El Parador.

Serves 4

3 large **sweet potatoes**, peeled and cut into slices 3cm thick

garlic-infused olive oil (see page 10)

Maldon sea salt and **cracked black pepper**, to taste

3 **red onions**, cut into quarters

1 heaped tablespoon **pinenuts**

75g **feta cheese**

Preheat your oven to 200°C/400°F/gas mark 6.

Put the sweet potatoes in a large roasting tray and drizzle generously with garlic oil until they are well coated. Sprinkle with 2 generous pinches of pepper and 3 of salt and mix well. Place in the middle of the oven for about an hour, or until the potatoes are tender, stirring every so often to ensure they don't burn.

Meanwhile, put the onion quarters in a small roasting tray, drizzle with garlic oil and season with a pinch of salt and pepper. Place them in the bottom of the oven and cook for 20 minutes.

While the sweet potatoes and onions are roasting, get a small frying pan and put it on a low heat. Do not add oil. Drop in the pinenuts and fry them gently, stirring constantly so they do not burn, until light golden brown. Tip straight away into a clean dish and leave to one side.

When the sweet potatoes and onions are ready, take them out of the oven and reduce the heat to 150°C/300°F/gas mark 2. Place a large, heavy-based, non-stick frying pan on a medium to high heat and pour in 5 dashes of garlic oil. Drop in half the roasted sweet potatoes and fry them for a few minutes until they start to break up. Add half the roasted onions and give everything a good stir. Cook for a further 5 minutes, stirring all the time to avoid anything burning, and then spoon the mixture into an ovenproof dish. Cover with foil and place in the oven while you fry the second batch of sweet potatoes and onions.

When the second batch is almost ready, add the first batch back to the pan and reduce the heat to low. Carefully stir in the pinenuts and feta cheese and continue cooking until the feta begins to melt. Serve straight away.

Remolacha Asada con Castañas

Roasted beetroot pan-fried with chestnuts, roasted red onions, chilli oil and balsamic vinegar

Beetroot is often given short shift because people have bad memories of eating over-vinegary beetroot at some time in their lives. At El Parador we must be doing something right, because the beetroot dishes we put on the menu always seem to please.

Serves 4

3 large **beetroots**, washed

Maldon sea salt and **cracked black pepper**, to taste

chilli-infused olive oil (see page 10)

3 **red onions**, cut into quarters

8 **roasted chestnuts**, shelled (most delis sell vacuum-packed packets of pre-roasted chestnuts if you don't have fresh)

balsamic vinegar

Preheat your oven to 190ºC/375ºF/gas mark 5.

Drop the beetroots into a large pan of salted water and bring to the boil. Turn the heat down and simmer, uncovered, for 3 hours. Drain, allow to cool slightly, and then peel off the skins. Cut each beetroot in half, then into slices 3cm thick. Place in a roasting tray, drizzle liberally with chilli oil and sprinkle with 2 generous pinches of salt and 1 of pepper. Roast in the oven for 25 minutes, then transfer to a clean bowl and leave to one side.

Meanwhile, put the onion quarters in a small roasting tray, drizzle with garlic oil and season with a pinch of salt and pepper. Place them in the bottom of the oven and cook for 20 minutes.

Lightly crush the chestnuts using a pestle and mortar.

When everything is out of the oven, turn it down to 150ºC/300ºF/gas mark 2. Place a large, heavy-based, non-stick frying pan on a medium heat and pour in 8 dashes of chilli oil. When it begins to smoke, drop in half the roasted beetroot and 2 generous pinches of pepper and salt. Cook for 3 minutes, or until the beetroot starts to darken, stirring occasionally. Add half the roasted onions, a dash of balsamic and half the chestnuts, and cook together for a further 3 minutes. Spoon into an ovenproof dish, cover with foil, and place in the oven to keep warm while you get on with the second batch. Just before the second batch is ready, return the first batch to the pan, drizzle with 2 dashes of chilli oil and toss together for a minute to heat everything through. Serve straight away.

Alcachofas del Parador

Artichoke hearts pan-fried with chicory leaves, oregano and caramelised onions

One of my many lasting memories of my gran was watching her eat raw artichoke stems. After she had whipped me up my egg and chips for lunch, she would move on to prepare the evening meal. If we were going to be having artichokes later, she would sit down with me while I ate my lunch and calmly slice off bits from the artichoke's stem to eat with bread for her lunch – nothing else. I would have scoffed all my egg and chips in the time it took her to get halfway down the stem. 'Porque tanta prisa?', she would say, 'what's the hurry?' She couldn't quite grasp the urgency of a nine year old who wanted to get back on the football pitch.

Serves 4

8 **marinated artichoke hearts** (preferably with long stems), cut in half
3 **garlic cloves**, finely chopped
extra virgin olive oil, to marinate the artichokes
Maldon sea salt and **cracked black pepper**
olive oil
1 small **onion**, finely chopped
3 sprigs **fresh oregano leaves**, discard the stalks
1 head of **chicory**, cut into slices 1cm thick

First prepare the artichoke hearts. Place your griddle plate, ridged-side up, on a high heat. When it's smoking hot, put on the artichoke quarters and let them char until the ridge marks are heavily defined on both sides – press down on them with a spatula, if it helps. Transfer the charred artichokes to a bowl with the chopped garlic, 7 dashes of extra virgin olive oil and 2 pinches of pepper and salt. Mix well, cover the bowl with clingfilm and leave in the fridge to marinate for 2 hours.

Place a large, heavy-based, non-stick frying pan on a low heat with 9 dashes of olive oil. Add the onion, oregano and 2 pinches of salt and black pepper, and then fry them gently, stirring regularly, until the onion is soft and golden. Remove with a slotted spoon and place in a dish to one side.

Return the pan to a medium heat and add the grilled and marinated artichoke hearts and the fried onion. Cook until the artichokes are heated right through, add the chicory, season to taste with salt and pepper, and then give everything a final stir to heat it through evenly. Serve with the bread of your choice.

Alcachofas con Habas Verdes y Espinacas

Grilled marinated artichoke hearts pan-fried with broad beans,
spinach and chillies

The pale green of the charred artichokes, the bright green of the broad beans and the rich green of the spinach are all cut by the red of the chilli peppers. All the flavours are clean and distinguishable. A lovely, simple dish. For variation, you can replace the chillies with $1/2$ teaspoon harissa paste, mixed with 50ml olive oil, and stirred in with the broad beans.

Serves 4

8 **marinated artichoke hearts** (preferably with long stems), cut in half

3 **garlic cloves**, finely chopped

extra virgin olive oil, to marinate the artichokes

500g fresh, **young leaf spinach**, washed (and prepared as on page 114)

olive oil

Maldon sea salt and **cracked black pepper**, to taste

16–20 frozen **broad beans** (husks removed), defrosted

2 medium **red chillies**, deseeded and finely sliced

Chargrill the artichoke hearts and marinate them in garlic and extra virgin olive oil (see opposite page).

Meanwhile, prepare and cook the spinach (see page 114).

Once everything is ready, place a large, heavy-based, non-stick frying pan on a medium/high heat with 8 dashes of olive oil. When the oil is smoking hot, drop in the artichokes and season with a generous pinch of salt. Cook for 3 minutes, stirring regularly, and then add the cooked spinach and cook for 1 minute more. Drop in the broad beans and sliced chillies and stir-fry together for $1^1/2$ minutes and serve.

Espárragos con Alcachofas

Asparagus and artichoke hearts pan-fried with peas, mint and coriander

Artichokes go very well with asparagus.

Serves 4

6 **marinated artichoke hearts** (preferably with long stems), cut into quarters

3 **garlic cloves**, finely chopped

extra virgin olive oil, to marinate the artichokes

16 large **asparagus spears**, trimmed at the base

olive oil

2 sprigs **fresh mint**, coarsely chopped

3 sprigs **fresh coriander**, coarsely chopped

Maldon sea salt and **cracked black pepper**, to taste

1 handful **frozen garden peas**, defrosted

Chargrill the artichoke hearts and marinate them in garlic and extra virgin olive oil (see Solomillo con Alcachofas, page 66).

Place the asparagus in a pan of salted, boiling water and cook for 4–5 minutes or until they are just tender but still retain a bit of bite. Drain and leave to one side.

Place your griddle plate on a high heat, ridged-side up, and allow it to get smoking hot. Lay the asparagus on top and chargrill until there are scorch marks all over them.

Meanwhile, heat a large, heavy-based, non-stick frying pan over a medium to high heat with 8 dashes of olive oil. When it is smoking hot, drop in the artichokes, asparagus, fresh mint and fresh coriander. Season with 2 generous pinches of pepper and 1 of salt, and then stir-fry together for 3 minutes. Add the peas and cook for a further minute to heat through. Serve straight away.

Ensalada de Remolacha Asada

Roasted beetroot salad with French beans, feta cheese and radicchio

The sweet beetroot in this salad blends well with the creaminess of the cheese and the slight bitterness of the radicchio.

Serves 4

3 large **beetroots**

20 **French beans**, trimmed and blanched in boiling water until tender

salad dressing of your choice (one of our favourites is the dressing on page 141, for Setas a la Plancha)

15 **radicchio leaves**, washed and coarsely torn

75g **feta cheese**

chilli-infused olive oil (see page 10)

Maldon sea salt and **cracked black pepper**, to taste

Prepare and roast the beetroot as you would for the Remolacha Asada con Castanas on page 120. When done, take out of the oven and allow to cool.

Pour 3 tablespoons of your preferred dressing into a large salad bowl. Add the roasted beetroot, French beans and radicchio leaves, and then crumble over the feta cheese. Add a further spoonful of dressing, dig in with both hands and combine everything together. Adjust the seasoning, if necessary, and serve.

Salteado de Espárragos y Judías Verdes

Asparagus and French beans pan-fried with chilli oil and toasted pinenuts

Here is a lovely recipe that combines French beans and asparagus.

Serves 4

12 large **asparagus spears**, trimmed at the base

Maldon sea salt and **cracked black pepper**, to taste

250g **French beans**, trimmed and blanched in boiling water until tender

1 tablespoon **pinenuts**

chilli-infused olive oil (see page 10)

40g **butter**

juice of 1/2 **lemon**

Place the asparagus in a pan of salted, boiling water and cook for 4–5 minutes, or until they are just tender but still retain a bit of bite. Remove with a slotted spoon and leave to one side with the French beans.

Place a small, dry frying pan on a low heat. Drop in the pinenuts and fry very gently, stirring regularly and watching them all the time, until they start to change colour. Remove from the heat immediately and tip into a dish and leave to one side.

Heat a large, heavy-based, non-stick frying pan over a low heat with 12 dashes of chilli oil. When the oil is smoking hot, turn the heat to medium and add the butter. Allow the butter to melt and sizzle, and then squeeze in the lemon juice. Add the asparagus, French beans and a generous pinch of salt, and then turn up the heat to high and cook fiercely for 3 minutes, stirring all the time. Add the pinenuts and toss for a further 40 seconds.

Judías Verdes al Moruno

French beans pan-fried with caramelised onions, garlic, cumin and coriander

Elizabeth David once said that she would rather 'eat a dish of tiny green beans in the early summer that go to the money and trouble that asparagus entails…' I know a lot of people who do not like French beans because they say that they have no flavour. I cannot disagree with them more! Cooked properly, that is, just slightly crunchy to the bite, they are delicious – even overcooked, they're still lovely. I was brought up on overcooked beans and other vegetables – that's how my parents cooked them, adding lovely herbs and oils to them, serving them hot or cold. It is only as my palate developed that I came to prefer them slightly crunchier.

Serves 4

350g **French beans**, trimmed and blanched in boiling water until tender

Maldon sea salt and **cracked black pepper**, to taste

olive oil

1 **Spanish onion**, finely sliced

3 **garlic cloves**, finely sliced

$1/2$ teaspoon **cumin seeds**, crushed

$1/2$ teaspoon **coriander seeds**, crushed

4 **lime wedges**, to serve

Place a large, heavy-based, non-stick frying pan on a low heat with 12 dashes of olive oil. Add the onions, garlic and 2 generous pinches of black pepper and fry gently until the onion is soft and golden. Remove with a slotted spoon and leave to one side.

Return the pan to a high heat and drop in the French beans. Season with a pinch of salt and cook for 1 minute. Add the cumin and coriander seeds and cook for a further 2 minutes, stirring regularly. Finally, put in the fried garlic and onions and stir-fry together for 2 minutes more. Serve straight away with some lime wedges on the side.

Brécol del Parador

Broccoli pan-fried with baby carrots, roasted cherry tomatoes, pumpkin seeds, harissa and cumin oil

Broccoli has to rank as one of our favourite vegetables. It tastes great as a course on its own with a little olive oil drizzled over it, or tossed in some warm butter and lots of black pepper, and it goes well with either fish or meat. At El Parador we cook it in many ways, but this is one of our three favourites.

Serves 4

olive oil

1/2 teaspoon **cumin powder**

1/4 teaspoon **harissa paste**

Maldon sea salt and **cracked black pepper**, to taste

1 tablespoon **pumpkin seeds**

300g **broccoli**, cut into medium florets

12 **baby carrots** (stems on)

12 **cherry tomatoes**, roasted in olive oil and salt at 150°C/300°F/gas mark 2 for 1 hour, or until soft

Pour 100ml of olive oil into a measuring jug, and then stir in the cumin and harissa with a pinch of salt and pepper. Combine well and leave to infuse.

Place a small, dry frying pan on a low heat. Allow it to heat up, and then add the pumpkin seeds. Stir them around in the pan and watch them as they start to brown. Just before they begin to pop, as some will, tip them into a dish and leave to one side.

Bring a large pan of water to the boil with 2 pinches of salt. Drop in the broccoli and carrots and cook for 3–4 minutes, or until just tender but still with a bit of bite. Drain thoroughly and leave to one side.

Place a large, heavy-based, non-stick frying pan on a high heat with the infused harissa and cumin oil. When it is hot, drop in the broccoli and carrots and cook for 30 seconds – don't worry if they start to colour. Add the roasted tomatoes and continue to cook for a further 30 seconds. Just before you are about to serve, toss in the toasted seeds and mix well together.

Brécol con Tomatitos, Aceitunas y Alcaparras

Broccoli pan-fried with roasted cherry tomatoes, olives and capers

The tomatoes, olives and capers here blend to give a rich flavour, yet do not overpower the intrinsic flavour of the broccoli.

Serves 4

400g **broccoli**, cut into medium florets

Maldon sea salt and **cracked black pepper**, to taste

garlic-infused olive oil (see page 10)

12 **cherry tomatoes**, roasted in olive oil and salt at 150°C/300°F/gas mark 2 for 1 hour, or until soft

10 good-quality **black olives** (stones removed), coarsely chopped

12 **capers**

2 sprigs **flat-leaf parsley**, coarsely chopped

Bring a large pan of water to the boil with 2 pinches of salt. Drop in the broccoli and cook for 3–4 minutes, or until tender but with a bit of crunch. Drain thoroughly and leave to one side.

Place a large, heavy-based, non-stick frying pan on a low heat with 12 dashes of garlic oil and 2 pinches of black pepper. When the oil is hot, put in the roasted tomatoes and cook gently for 1 minute. Add the olives and capers, cook together for a further 2 minutes, stirring all the time. Remove everything with a slotted spoon and place in a dish on one side.

Return the pan to a high heat and add the broccoli and a pinch of salt and stir-fry until the broccoli has heated through. Return the tomatoes, olives and capers to the pan, sprinkle over the parsley, and cook together for a further 2 minutes, stirring all the time.

Brécol con Achicoria Roja

Broccoli pan-fried with red endive, spring onions and toasted sesame seeds

The bitterness of the endive marries well with the sweetness of the spring onions in this dish.

Serves 4

400g **broccoli**, cut into medium florets

Maldon sea salt and **cracked black pepper**, to taste

1 tablespoon **sesame seeds**

garlic-infused olive oil (see page 10)

20g **butter**

2 medium **spring onions**, cut into slices 5mm thick

1 head **red endive** (chicory), cut into slices 1cm thick

Bring a large pan of water to the boil with 2 pinches of salt. Drop in the broccoli and cook for 3–4 minutes, or until tender but still with a bit of bite. Drain thoroughly and set aside.

Place a small, dry frying pan on a low heat. When it is hot, put in the sesame seeds and fry them very gently, stirring continuously, until they start to change colour. Tip them immediately into a clean dish and leave to one side.

Place a large, heavy-based, non-stick frying pan on a low heat with 12 dashes of garlic oil. When the oil is hot, drop in the butter and season with 2 pinches of black pepper. Allow the butter to melt and sizzle, and then add the spring onions. Fry gently until soft and golden brown. Remove with a slotted spoon and place in a dish to one side.

Turn the heat up to high and drop in the broccoli. Stir-fry until it has heated through, and then add the spring onions. Cook together for 1 minute, stirring regularly. Add the endive and stir-fry for a further minute, and then stir in the sesame seeds and cook for 1 minute more. Serve straight away.

Espinacas con Garbanzos y Cebollas

Pan-fried spinach with chickpeas, caramelised red onions, garlic and cherry tomatoes

I was hooked on spinach right from my first episode of Popeye. This is our favourite recipe, and most parts of Spain have their own regional variation.

Serves 4

olive oil

800g fresh, **young leaf spinach**, washed

Maldon sea salt and **cracked black pepper**, to taste

1 large **garlic clove**, finely sliced

2 medium **red onions**, finely sliced

12 **cherry tomatoes**, roasted in olive oil and salt at 150°C/300°F/gas mark 2 for 1 hour, or until soft

1 x 400g tin/jar **chickpeas**, drained

Place a large, heavy-based frying pan (or wok) on a high heat with 2 dashes of olive oil. When the oil is smoking hot, put in the spinach, add a pinch of salt and turn the leaves gently in the pan until they start to wilt. Just as the spinach starts to release its water, remove the pan from the heat and tip the spinach into a bowl lined with kitchen paper to soak up the bitter cooking juices. (If your pan isn't big enough, you may have to cook the spinach in 2 hits, in which case make sure you wipe out the pan, re-oil it and get the oil good and hot before you add the second lot of spinach.)

Clean the pan and return it to a low heat with 12 dashes of olive oil. When it is hot, put in the garlic, onions, 2 pinches of pepper and 1 of salt. Fry until the garlic and onions are soft and golden. Remove with a slotted spoon and place in a dish to one side.

Return the pan to a medium/high heat. Put in the cooked spinach with a generous pinch of salt and cook until the spinach is hot, stirring all the time. Return the garlic and onions to the pan, along with the roasted tomatoes, and cook together for 1 minute, stirring. Tip in the chickpeas and cook for a further 2 minutes, or until heated through, and serve.

Empanadillas de Queso y Espinacas

Spinach and cheese parcels

Here is the vegetarian version of the Empanadillas de Atun (see page 31). Patrick used to work in a restaurant many moons ago where they served something similar. We tried it, experimented with different cheeses, and it has been a firm favourite ever since.

Serves 4–6

for the filling

800g fresh, **young leaf spinach**, washed

100g good-quality, **full-fat cream cheese**

100g **mature Cheddar cheese**, grated

Maldon sea salt and **cracked black pepper**, to taste

olive oil

for the pastry

1 packet ready-rolled **puff pastry**

1 beaten **egg**

Place a large, heavy-based frying pan (or wok) on a high heat with 2 dashes of olive oil. When the oil is smoking hot, put in the spinach, add a pinch of salt and turn the leaves gently in the pan until they start to wilt. Just as the spinach starts to release its water, remove the pan from the heat and tip the spinach into a bowl lined with kitchen paper to soak up the bitter cooking juices. Allow it to cool, and then tip it into a large mixing bowl. Add both the cheeses and season with 2 pinches of pepper and 1 of salt. Mix everything together really well, and then cover the bowl with clingfilm and place in the fridge for 2 hours.

Preheat your oven to 200°C/400°F/gas mark 6.

Lightly flour your worksurface and place the rolled puff pastry on top. Using a sharp knife, cut the pastry into 12cm squares and arrange them on several greased baking sheets. You will need 8–12 depending on how many people you are serving. Gauge it so you have enough pastry to wrap the filling. If the pastry is too thin, the parcel will burst and all the ingredients will spill out. Some spillage is fine. If the pastry is too thick, it will not allow the flavours of the filling to come through.

Put a dollop of the cold cheese and spinach filling, a ball shape roughly 5–6cm in diameter, in the middle of the square, and then dab the edges of the square with beaten egg. Bring up the corners of the pastry to the centre and press them together to form a peak at the top. Glaze the tops with beaten egg, and then bake in the oven for 15 minutes, or until golden brown. Serve hot or at room temperature.

Pimientos de Padrón

Padron peppers pan-fried with virgin olive oil and sea salt

'Pimientos de Padrón' are small, green peppers that come from Galicia in northwest Spain. They are roughly the size of your thumb and look like green chillies, but are more wrinkled. Some have the savoury sweetness of green peppers, but the odd one has a bit of a kick to it. We like to serve them as a dish on their own, and the curious thing is that you can be merrily munching away… and then you get a hot one. It won't take your head off, but it'll definitely take your breath away and leave you grabbing for your beer to temper the heat… and then you'll go back for more. My nephew Solomon was five years old when he had his first Padron pepper in Majorca. It was a hot one and it brought tears to his eyes, but he still laps them up whenever he comes to El Parador.

Serves 4

extra virgin olive oil
30 **Padron green peppers**
Maldon sea salt, to taste

Try and do this in one hit. However, if your pan's not big enough, serve the first batch while the second one is cooking.

Place a large, heavy-based frying pan (or wok) on a high heat with 3 dashes of extra virgin olive oil. When the oil starts to smoke, toss in the peppers whole with 2 generous pinches of sea salt. The salt plays an important part – it is the catalyst that enhances the flavour of the peppers. As soon as the skins start to brown, tip into a bowl and serve straight away.

Huevos Fritos con Ajo y Pimientos de Padrón

Fried eggs with garlic and Padron peppers

When I was about nine or ten years old, my grandmother used to cook lunch for me throughout the week during the school holidays. I used to eat fried egg and chips every time – wolf them down and then shoot off to play football in the park. My gran could knock up a mean egg and chips. The eggs would be fried in good olive oil that had chunks of garlic in it, all nicely golden, then the egg would cook around them. The chips were cut by hand – sometimes thin, sometimes chunkier – depending, I think, on how she felt, and shallow-fried in olive oil. I liked to dunk some of the chips in my egg yolk until it was finished, then I would chop up the egg, douse the chips in ketchup, mix the whole thing up and devour it.

A few months ago, I was eating in a local café in Barcelona and on the menu was egg and chips. So, I thought, why not? The waiter came along with the egg and chips in a pan, dashed it with olive oil and ketchup, chopped it all up and served it on my plate. Two things happened in my head. One, I nearly cried because I was immediately transported back to my grandmother's kitchen, and two, I was relieved that I was not such a weird kid after all, by chopping up my egg and chips!

At El Parador, we don't go the whole hog with the chips – but we do fry a mean egg.

Serves 4

olive oil

4 large **garlic cloves** (1 for each egg), coarsely chopped

12 **Padron green peppers** (3 for each egg)

Maldon sea salt and **cracked black pepper**, to taste

4 **eggs** (duck eggs are worth trying for a change – they're really rich and creamy)

You'll have to do this in 2 hits, unless you have a very large, heavy-based frying pan. Let's assume you do. Pour in a large amount of olive oil, about 2.5cm deep in the pan. When it's hot, add the chopped garlic and the whole peppers. Do not forget to add 2 generous pinches of salt and pepper. Stir the garlic and peppers around so they release as much of their flavour as possible into the olive oil. When they start to brown, remove them immediately with a slotted spoon and leave to one side. Crack the eggs, one at a time, into the same pan with the same oil. As the whites start to solidify, carefully scatter the fried garlic and peppers among the eggs so each has its fair share. Then cook as you would like your eggs. When they're done, serve with some lovely bread... some chips... and a dollop of ketchup.

Setas al Marroquin

Flat mushrooms pan-fried with garlic and served with harissa and parsley

Mushrooms are one of those vegetables that you mature into liking. As a child, I hated them. They were especially horrible in school dinners (so was cabbage). I think it's fair to say that school dinners are responsible for blunting a lot of people's taste buds. My two teenage children have no desire for mushrooms, however much I try to entice them.

Serves 4

100ml **olive oil**

3 large whole **garlic cloves**, unpeeled and lightly crushed with the flat of a knife

Maldon sea salt and **cracked black pepper**, to taste

1/2 teaspoon **harissa paste** (see page 11)

1 small bunch **flat-leaf parsley**, roughly chopped

400g **flat mushrooms**

Pour 75ml of olive oil into a heavy-based frying pan (or wok) and place on a medium heat. Add 1¹/₂ of the garlic cloves, crushed with the skin on, and a pinch of salt and pepper. Let the garlic brown slowly, stirring well, and then pour the flavoured oil into a jug and stir in the harissa paste and half of the chopped parsley. Place to one side.

Preheat your oven to 150°C/300°F/gas mark 2.

Gently clean the mushrooms and chop roughly. Unless the large pan (or wok) you have previously used can take all the mushrooms, you will have to do this in 2 hits. Heat the remaining 25ml of olive oil. Peel and thinly slice the remaining cloves of garlic. Add half of them to the pan and fry very gently until they begin to brown. Now add half the chopped mushrooms, a generous pinch of salt and pepper and a pinch of chopped parsley. Sauté gently over a low to medium heat, stirring occasionally, until the mushrooms are lovely and soft. Spoon into an ovenproof dish, drizzle over some of the flavoured oil you have just made and season with a pinch more salt. Cover with foil and place in the bottom of the oven to keep warm while you fry up the second batch of mushrooms.

Once all the mushrooms are cooked, spoon them into a serving bowl and mix well together. To finish, stir the remaining parsley into the jug of warm, flavoured oil and drizzle over the mushrooms. This is an oily dish, but the oil will be flavoured enough to entice you to mop it up with some bread afterwards.

Setas con Salsa Picante

Chestnut mushrooms pan-fried with a tomato, garlic and red chilli sauce

We love the taste of chestnut mushrooms. Once they soften and soak up the juices from the tomatoes, garlic and chilli they taste even better. At the end of the cooking process, try scrambling an egg into it – it makes a great veggie fry-up.

Serves 4

8 **cherry tomatoes,** roasted in olive oil and salt at 150°C/300°F/gas mark 2 for 1 hour, or until soft

5 **red chillies**

4 **garlic cloves**, use the garlic from the garlic confit on page 10

olive oil

Maldon sea salt and **cracked black pepper**, to taste

50g **butter**

500g **chestnut mushrooms**, cleaned and cut in half

2 sprigs **flat-leaf parsley**, coarsely chopped

While the tomatoes are roasting, put the chillies onto skewers and hold them over a naked flame on the stove until the skins turn black (wear oven gloves for this, because the skewers will get hot). Cut off the stalks, remove the seeds and place the chillies in the roasting tray with the tomatoes for the final 10 minutes of cooking.

When the tomatoes/chillies are ready, place them in a food-processor with the garlic. Add 100ml of olive oil and 2 pinches of salt, and then blend to a smooth sauce, the consistency of single cream. Add more oil, if necessary.

Put a large, heavy-based, non-stick frying pan (or wok) on a medium heat with 10 dashes of olive oil. When it is hot, add one-third of the butter and a pinch of pepper. Allow the butter to melt and sizzle, and then put in one-third of the mushrooms. Patiently sauté the mushrooms until they soften, stirring regularly. Place in a dish and leave to one side. Fry the remaining mushrooms in two batches, following the same method.

When all the mushrooms are done, clean the pan and put it back on a medium heat with 6 dashes of olive oil. When it is hot, put in the cooked mushrooms and fry them together for 2 minutes. Season to taste with salt and pepper. Spoon the pepper sauce over the mushrooms and stir in the parsley. Cook for 2 minutes, and then serve.

Setas a la Plancha

Grilled oyster mushrooms drizzled with olive oil, garlic, rosemary, lemon and sesame seeds

Oyster mushrooms have a great meaty flavour and texture. I don't like them fried in oil because they end up tasting slimy, but their flavour really comes out when they're cooked 'dry' on a griddle.

Serves 4

1 tablespoon **sesame seeds**

about 20 **oyster mushrooms**, with heads roughly the size of a tennis ball

for the dressing

175ml **olive oil**

3 large **garlic cloves**, left whole and crushed

Maldon sea salt and **cracked black pepper**, to taste

2 sprigs **fresh rosemary**

1/2 **lemon**

First make the dressing. Pour the oil into a heavy-based frying pan and put it on a low to medium heat. When the oil is hot, put in the garlic cloves and stir gently for 20 seconds. Turn down the heat to low, add a couple of pinches of pepper and salt, and allow the garlic to cook slowly until it just starts to brown. Add the sprigs of rosemary and continue cooking until the garlic turns golden brown. Pour into a bowl, adjust the seasoning and leave to cool. When the dressing has cooled down, drop in the unsqueezed lemon half, cover with clingfilm and leave to mature for 24 hours at room temperature.

Meanwhile, place a small dry frying pan on a low heat, add the sesame seeds and toast until they just start to change colour – you will have to keep an eye on them – gently shaking the pan occasionally so they are evenly toasted. Tip into a dish and leave to cool.

When you are ready to cook, place your large griddle on a high heat. Oil a piece of kitchen paper and lightly grease the surface to prevent the mushrooms sticking to it. When the griddle is smoking hot, lay on the mushrooms, sprinkle with a couple of pinches of salt, and cook until they start to darken – if necessary, press down on them with a spatula to ensure they make contact with the griddle.

When they are done, arrange them on a large plate, drizzle over some of the dressing and sprinkle with the toasted sesame seeds.

Hinojo Asado con Espinacas

Roasted fennel pan-fried with spinach, pinenuts, tarragon and chilli oil

Fennel is such a versatile vegetable that lends itself to being cooked or used in salads. Raw, the aniseed flavour predominates, although you can subdue its flavour with a good, tart dressing. Cooked fennel has a less pronounced flavour. We like to roast it first, and then pan-fry it with other ingredients.

Serves 4

6 medium **fennel bulbs**

Maldon sea salt and **cracked black pepper**, to taste

garlic-infused olive oil (see page 10)

olive oil

300g fresh **young leaf spinach**, washed

chilli-infused olive oil (see page 10)

1 heaped tablespoon **pinenuts**

sprig of **fresh tarragon**, coarsely chopped

Preheat your oven to 220°C/425°F/gas mark 7. Cut the fennel bulbs into quarters and place them in a pan of boiling water with 2 generous pinches of salt. Bring to the boil, and then simmer until just becoming tender. Drain, and then place in a roasting tray with 8 dashes of garlic oil and 2 pinches of salt and pepper. Roast on the middle shelf of the oven for 45 minutes, turning regularly, or until charred (but not burnt!). Remove from the oven, tip into a bowl and place to one side. Turn the oven down to 150°C/300°F/gas mark 2.

Place a large, heavy-based pan (or wok) on a high heat with 2 dashes of olive oil. When the oil is smoking hot, put in the spinach, add a pinch of salt and turn the leaves gently in the pan until they start to wilt. Just as the spinach starts to release its water, remove the pan from the heat and tip the spinach into a bowl lined with kitchen paper to soak up the bitter cooking juices. (If your pan isn't big enough, you may have to cook it in 2 hits, in which case make sure you wipe out the pan, re-oil it and get the oil good and hot before you do the second lot.)

Clean the pan and return it to the hob on a high heat. Pour in 8 dashes of chilli oil and, when it's hot, spoon in half the roasted fennel. Cook for 3 minutes, stirring well, then toss in half the pinenuts and continue to cook for a further 15 seconds. Finally, add half the spinach, a generous pinch of tarragon, a pinch of salt and 2 pinches of pepper. Cook for a further 30 seconds, stirring all the time. Spoon into an ovenproof dish, cover in foil, and place in the oven to keep warm while you cook the second batch. Just before the second one is ready, return the first batch to the pan and carefully mix everything together.

Hinojo del Parador

Roasted fennel pan-fried with lime, garlic and Manchego cheese

Another dish here with sharp clean flavours. Try not to put too much cheese on it as this could dull it. The lime contrasts with the sweet nuttiness of the garlic and the aniseed flavour of the fennel.

Serves 4

6 medium **fennel bulbs** (prepare as in recipe opposite)

olive oil

3 **garlic cloves**, use the garlic from the garlic confit on page 10

Maldon sea salt and **cracked black pepper**, to taste

juice of 1 **lime**

1 handful of **Manchego cheese**, grated

Prepare the fennel as in the recipe opposite, but substitute the infused oil with normal olive oil. When the fennel is ready, place a large, heavy-based, non-stick frying pan on a medium heat with 8 dashes of olive oil. Add the garlic and stir for 1 minute, then add the fennel, a generous pinch of salt and 2 pinches of pepper. Stir-fry everything together for 3 minutes, and then squeeze in the lime juice. Finally, add the Manchego cheese and toss for a further minute.

Hinojo con Tomatitos, Garbanzos, Salvia y Manteca

Roasted fennel pan-fried with cherry tomatoes, chickpeas and sage

Here are four flavours that all combine and work well with each other.

Serves 4

6 medium **fennel bulbs** (prepare as in recipe opposite)

olive oil

50g **butter**

juice of 1/2 **lemon**

2 sprigs **fresh sage**

12 **cherry tomatoes**, roasted as on page 25

Maldon sea salt and **cracked black pepper**, to taste

400g tin/jar **chickpeas**, drained

Prepare and roast the fennel as in the recipe opposite. Place a large, heavy-based, non-stick frying pan on a low heat with 10 dashes of olive oil. When it is hot, drop in the butter. Allow the butter to melt and sizzle, and then squeeze in the lemon juice and add the sage. Cook for 1 minute, to allow the flavour of the sage to infuse the oil, and then add the roasted tomatoes, 2 generous pinches of pepper and 1 of salt. Cook for 2 minutes, stirring all the time, and then add the fennel and chickpeas. Cook for a further 3 minutes, stirring regularly, and then serve.

Parrillada de Calabazas

Courgettes and butternut squash pan-fried with oregano, goat's cheese and garlic oil

Courgettes and butternut squash make a wonderful colour combination. Put some goat's cheese and oregano in with them and you have a tasty dish. If only it was that simple! Well, it is really.

Serves 4

2 **butternut squash**, peeled and cut into quarters

garlic-infused olive oil (see page 10)

Maldon sea salt and **cracked black pepper**, to taste

3 sprigs **fresh oregano leaves**, roughly chopped (stalks removed)

4 large **courgettes**, cut in half lengthways, then in half again and sprinkled with salt to draw out the excess water

75g **soft goat's cheese**

Place the peeled and quartered butternut squash in a roasting tray. Drizzle over enough garlic oil to coat them and sprinkle with 3 generous pinches of pepper, 2 of salt and most of the oregano (reserve 2 pinches for the courgettes). Place the tray in the oven and roast for 50 minutes, turning occasionally.

Meanwhile, place your griddle plate, ridged-side up, on a high heat. When it is smoking hot, lay the courgettes on top and grill them until they start to soften and blacken. Transfer them to a dish and sprinkle over the remaining oregano.

Once the squash is cooked, place a large, heavy-based, non-stick frying pan (or wok) on a medium to high heat with 10 dashes of garlic oil. When it is smoking hot, put in the chargrilled courgettes and roasted squash and fry them together for 4 minutes or until they start to brown. Crumble in the goat's cheese, season with 1 generous pinch of pepper, and continue to cook for a further 2 minutes, stirring all the time, until the cheese begins to melt. Serve straight away.

Calabacines con Tomillo

Braised courgettes pan-fried with butter and thyme

I first enjoyed this dish in a small bar in the Cévennes region of France. My wife had rabbit (which was fantastic) and I opted for the steak and chips, but it was the courgettes that really surprised me – all soft and buttery, with a hint of olive oil and a lovely aroma of thyme.

Serves 4

4 large **courgettes**, cut into slices 2.5cm thick

Maldon sea salt and **cracked black pepper**, to taste

olive oil

40g **butter**

2 sprigs **fresh thyme**, roughly chopped

Bring a pan of water to the boil with 2 generous pinches of salt. Put in the courgettes and cook for 1–2 minutes, or until they are just tender but still retain a bit of crunch. Drain.

Place a large, heavy-based, non-stick frying pan on a high heat with 7 dashes of olive oil and 2 pinches of pepper. When it is smoking hot, drop in the courgettes and stir-fry for 30 seconds. Add the butter and the thyme and cook until the butter starts to sizzle and the water has evaporated. Stir regularly, but avoid breaking up the courgettes. Serve straight away.

Ensalada de Pimientos Asados

Chargrilled pepper salad

My Auntie Anita is responsible for making the best salad I have ever tasted. It's clean flavours conjure up sitting in the warm evening sun… enjoying a few beers… tucking into it with some good, crusty bread… pretty much what I see when I look out into the garden terrace at El Parador… the voices and clunking of glasses rising up into the blue skies… you wouldn't think you were in Camden! It is amazing that tastes and smells can spark off so much nostalgia.

Serves 4

2 medium **green peppers**

2 medium **red peppers**

2 medium **yellow peppers** (optional, but they make a lovely colour combination)

2 firm, medium **tomatoes**

2 large **garlic cloves** (skins on)

100ml **extra virgin olive oil**

50ml **white wine vinegar**

Maldon sea salt and **cracked black pepper**, to taste

1 medium **onion**, finely sliced

Preheat your oven to 160°C/325°F/gas mark 3. Spike the peppers with skewers and hold them over a high flame on the stove until the skin is charred and black – wear oven gloves for this because the skewers will get hot. Leave the peppers to cool down slightly, and then peel off the skins. It helps if you wrap them in clingfilm first, which will make them sweat. When you have removed the skins, cut off the tops, remove the seeds and cut them into long, thin strips.

Place your griddle plate, ridged-side up, on a high heat. When it is smoking hot, lay on the peppers and scorch the flesh. Remove and place them in a long, deep-sided flat dish. Keep the griddle on the heat. Place the whole tomatoes on the griddle and char them until their skins blacken. Remove the skins and chop the flesh coarsely. Add them to the peppers. Keep the griddle on the heat. Repeat the chargrilling process with the garlic. Remove the scorched outer skins, and then slice them very finely. Add to the peppers and tomatoes.

To make the dressing, pour 100ml of olive oil into a large mixing bowl and whisk in the vinegar. Season to taste with salt and pepper. Pour the dressing over the peppers, tomatoes and garlic, add the raw onions and mix well so everything is well coated. Cover with clingfilm and refrigerate for 12 hours to infuse the flavours. Serve at room temperature with some lovely bread.

Col con Piñoñes al Ajillo

Savoy cabbage pan-fried with garlic, pinenuts and paprika

School dinners certainly put me off cabbage for a long time! When I re-discovered it, it was a lovely taste sensation.

Serves 6

1 large **Savoy cabbage** (or cabbage of your choice)

garlic-infused olive oil (see page 10)

1/2 teaspoon **sweet paprika**

3 **garlic cloves**, finely sliced

Maldon sea salt and **cracked black pepper**, to taste

75g **butter**

1 heaped tablespoon **pinenuts**

Preheat your oven to 150°C/300°F/gas mark 2. Pull the leaves off the cabbage, keeping as many of the outer, dark green leaves as possible. Discard the core. Coarsely tear the leaves, wash and put them in a pan of boiling water with 3 pinches of salt. Cook until they are tender but still with a bit of crunch, then drain thoroughly and place in a bowl to one side.

Pour 50ml of garlic oil into a measuring jug and stir in the paprika. Leave to infuse.

Place a large, heavy-based, non-stick frying pan (or wok) on a low heat with 12 dashes of garlic oil. Add the sliced garlic and 2 pinches of pepper, and then fry gently until the garlic is soft and golden. Pour the infused oil and the garlic into the jug with the paprika and mix well.

Return the pan to a high heat with half the garlic and paprika oil. When the oil is hot, drop in half the butter. Allow it to melt and sizzle, and then add half the cabbage with a pinch of salt. Stir-fry for 3 minutes, and then transfer to an ovenproof dish and place in the oven to keep warm. Cook the remaining cabbage in the same way. Just before the second batch of cabbage is ready, return the first batch to the pan with the pinenuts and cook together for 2 minutes. Serve straight away.

Espárragos del Mar con Alioli de Hinojo Asado

Samphire pan-fried with chilli oil and served with roasted fennel alioli

Samphire makes a great accompaniment to any grilled fish, but it can also be enjoyed on its own.

Serves 4

280g **samphire**, washed

chilli-infused olive oil (see page 10)

Maldon sea salt and **cracked black pepper**, to taste

for the roasted fennel alioli

2 **fennel heads**

6 tablespoons **Alioli** (see page 11)

Prepare and roast the fennel, as in the recipe Hinojo Asado con Espinacas (see page 142). When it's done, chop it up as finely as possible and combine it with 6 tablespoons of alioli. Cover and leave to mature in the fridge for 12 hours.

Place a large pan of water on a high heat and bring to the boil. When it is bubbling, drop in the samphire and stir for 30 seconds in the boiling water. Drain.

Place a large, heavy-based frying pan (or wok) on a medium heat and pour in 10 dashes of chilli oil. Turn the heat up a bit more and, as the oil begins to smoke, toss in the samphire and a pinch of salt. Cook for 40 seconds, stirring frequently so the samphire doesn't burn. When done, transfer to serving dishes and serve with a dollop of fennel alioli on each.

rice and lentils

When you think of Spain and rice, paella immediately springs to mind. The making of paella can take on ritualistic proportions as secret recipes handed down the family tree are adhered to. It is said that the original paella comes from Valencia on Spain's east coast, which might be true as it is the country's rice-growing region, but any Spaniard (myself included) will argue that the original, and best paella, was handed down to him by his forefathers.

The point is, you can put anything you want in paella. All paellas, regardless of where they come from in Spain, are 'joined at the hip' by the 'sofrito' (not by the saffron as it says in many books). The 'sofrito' is the caramelising of onions, garlic and peppers. The slow, gentle, patient frying of these three form the base flavour of any paella, and many other dishes. (My brother puts a finely chopped chicken liver in his.) There is also a rule that you do not stir the paella (un-like risottos) once the rice, stock and ingredients have reached simmering point – just gently shake the pan halfway through the process to prevent the rice from sticking. Once the rice is done and removed from the heat, leave it to stand, covered, for 5 minutes, to let the flavours settle.

Which rice to use? Well, a good rice is the calasparra rice which comes from Murcia. It is a short grain rice that has a good texture and can absorb liquid and flavours without falling apart. But whatever rice you use, it is the cooking process that matters. Another myth that my mother blew away was the necessity to use a 'paellera', the flat-based pans that you supposedly need to make 'true' paella. Any decent frying pan will do as long as it can take the volume of rice once it has absorbed the liquid you pour into it. So at El Parador when we cook rice we do not call it 'paella' we call it 'arroz', which simply means rice. We cook 'arroces' with meat, fish and vegetables. We also add butter and cheese on occasions, which brings them closer to an Italian risotto.

Paella Doña Ana

Paella

I would not be forgiven if I did not include my Aunt Anita's version of paella.

**Serves 4 as
a main course**

olive oil

4 **garlic cloves**, finely sliced

2 medium **onions**, finely sliced

2 large **tomatoes**, roughly chopped (you can seed and skin them if you wish)

2 large **red peppers**, finely sliced

1kg skinless **chicken breast**, cut into strips the length and thickness of your thumb

225g **squid**, cleaned and cut into rings (see page 47)

200g uncooked **tiger prawns** (defrosted), with heads and shells off

400g **fresh mussels** in their shells, cleaned and checked

300g **monkfish fillet**, cut into thin medallions

Maldon sea salt and **cracked black pepper**, to taste

100ml **white wine**

1 tablespoon **tomato purée**

300g **calasparra rice** (or paella rice of your choice)

1.5 litres **vegetable**, **fish** or **chicken stock** (or water)

pinch of **saffron strands**, soaked in 12ml hot water

2 **bay leaves**

1 handful **frozen garden peas**, defrosted

4 **lemon wedges**, to serve

Heat 12 dashes of olive oil in a large frying pan (or large, shallow casserole dish) on a low to medium heat. Add the garlic, onions, tomatoes and peppers and stir-fry very gently until the onions and garlic are caramelised, and the peppers are soft. Remove everything from the pan with a slotted spoon and place in a dish to one side.

Return the pan to a medium to high heat. Add the strips of chicken and stir-fry until light golden brown. Remove with a slotted spoon and place in a dish to one side.

Return the pan to a medium to high heat with 3 dashes of olive oil. Add the squid, prawns, mussels and monkfish and 2 pinches of salt and pepper. Pour in the wine, cover with a lid and cook until the mussels open. Remove the fish/seafood with a slotted spoon and place together in a dish to one side.

Keep the pan on the heat and stir in the tomato purée. Return all the cooked ingredients, except for the seafood, to the pan and stir well. Add the rice and stir it around to coat it in the oil. Pour over the stock and add 2 pinches of salt and 1 of pepper, the saffron and its water, and the bay leaves. Bring everything to the boil, give it one final stir, and then turn down the heat and simmer very gently for 20–30 minutes or until the rice is just cooked and the liquid is absorbed. Halfway through cooking, give the pan a couple of gentle, circular shakes to ensure the rice isn't sticking. Do not stir with a spoon. When the rice is cooked, take the pan off the heat and stir in the peas and the seafood. Season to taste with salt and pepper, cover with a lid and leave to stand for 5 minutes. Serve with lemon wedges on the side.

Arroz con Berenjenas

Calasparra rice with roasted aubergines, peas and mint

Roasted aubergines have a lovely creamy, nutty flavour that goes well with the texture of the rice. The hint of mint freshens the dish and the peas, as well as tasting nice, give it a lovely colour!

Serves 6 as a main course

2 large **aubergines**, cut in half lengthways

olive oil

garlic-infused olive oil

25g **butter** (optional)

Maldon sea salt and **cracked black pepper**, to taste

1kg **calasparra rice** (or rice of your choice)

1 litre **vegetable stock** (or water)

1 handful **frozen garden peas**, defrosted

2 sprigs **fresh mint**, coarsely chopped

1 handful **Manchego cheese**, grated (optional)

Preheat your oven to 200°C/400°F/gas mark 6.

Place the aubergines in a roasting tray, baste with some olive oil and roast in the oven for 15 minutes, or until the flesh is soft and brown. Allow to cool slightly, and then cut each half into slices 1.5cm thick.

Heat 8 dashes of garlic oil in a large frying pan on a low heat. Drop in the aubergine slices, half the butter (if using), 2 generous pinches of pepper and 1 of salt. Fry gently in the oil for 1 minute, and then add the rice. Stir well to coat it in the hot oil.

Pour over enough stock (or water) to cover the rice to a 1–2 finger width above the rice level and season to taste with salt and pepper. Bring to the boil, give the pan one final stir, and then turn down the heat and simmer very gently for 20–30 minutes until the rice is just cooked and the liquid is absorbed. Halfway through cooking, give the pan a couple of gentle, circular

Arroz del Mar

Calasparra rice with prawns, scallops, garlic and parsley

The clean flavours of the prawns and scallops combine with the nutty garlic and the fresh parsley to make this a simple but flavoursome rice dish.

Serves 6 as a main course

12 uncooked **tiger prawns** (defrosted), with heads off and shells on
olive oil
50g **butter**
juice of 1/2 **lemon**
3 large **garlic cloves**, thinly sliced
Maldon sea salt and **cracked black pepper**, to taste
8 **scallops**, cleaned and cut in half
1kg **calasparra rice** (or rice of your choice)
1 litre **vegetable stock** (or water)
3 sprigs **flat-leaf parsley**, coarsely chopped
6 **lemon wedges**, to serve

Using a sharp knife, carefully make an incision along the back of each prawn from the neck to the tail, remove the dark line along the spine and leave to one side.

Place a large, heavy-based, non-stick frying pan on a low heat with 12 dashes of olive oil and half the butter. Allow it to melt and sizzle, and then squeeze in the lemon juice. Add the garlic slices and fry them very gently until soft and starting to brown. Remove with a slotted spoon and place in a dish to one side.

Turn the heat up to medium, add the prawns and a pinch of salt and pepper, and then quickly sear them until their flesh turns pink – this will only take a few seconds. Remove them with a slotted spoon and place them with the garlic.

Lay the scallops in the pan and season with a pinch of salt and pepper. Sear for 1 minute on each side just to seal them, and then remove from the pan and place with the prawns and garlic.

Turn the heat down to low and allow the pan to cool slightly. Return the cooked ingredients to the pan and give everything a good stir. Add the rice, coating it in the oil and juices, and then pour over enough stock (or water) to cover the rice to a 1–2 finger width above the level of rice and season to taste with salt and pepper. Bring to the boil, give the rice one final stir, and then turn down the heat and simmer very gently for 20–30 minutes until the rice is just cooked and the liquid is absorbed. Halfway through cooking, give the pan a couple of gentle, circular shakes to ensure the rice isn't sticking. Do not stir with a spoon. When the rice is at the right consistency, take it off the heat, stir in the remaining butter and the parsley, and then leave to stand for 1–2 minutes with the lid on. Serve with lemon wedges on the side.

Lentejas de Doña Juana

Lentil and vegetable stew

My mum used to make some lovely lentil stews. Hearty things, that would warm you right through. They were a meal in themselves and I could not get enough of them. My mum would sit at the kitchen table, pour out the lentils, spread them out and then proceed to pick out any stones that had been collected with them thus avoiding anyone cracking their teeth when eating them. It was a labour of love to ensure the lentils would be delicious (which they always were) and when I was little she would sucker me into helping her by making a game out it. I soon cottoned on but as a young adult I would often help her and we would have a good old chat over it, sorting out the world's problems… well… mainly mine at the time!

Serves 4

olive oil

2 **garlic cloves**, finely sliced

1 small **red pepper**, finely sliced

1 small **green pepper**, finely sliced

1 large **Spanish onion**, finely sliced

Maldon sea salt and **cracked black pepper**, to taste

1 large **carrot**, peeled and cut into slices 1cm thick

8 medium **new potatoes**, washed and cut into slices 2cm thick

1 large stick of **celery**, cut into slices 1cm thick

400g **Puy lentils** (or lentils of your choice), washed

50g **long grain rice** (optional)

500ml **vegetable stock** (or water, if you have no stock to hand)

1 bay leaf

Place a casserole dish on a low heat with 10 dashes of olive oil. Put in the garlic, red and green peppers and onion, and season with a generous pinch of black pepper. Fry gently together for 10 minutes, stirring regularly, or until the vegetables are just starting to soften. Add the carrot, potatoes and celery and fry gently for a further 10 minutes, stirring regularly.

Add the lentils and rice (if using) and stir well for about a minute to coat them in the other ingredients. Pour over the stock (or water), topping up if necessary with more liquid so the level is 4cm above the level of the lentils/rice. Add the bay leaf and 2 pinches of salt and bring to the boil, then simmer for 45 minutes. Taste the lentils regularly to see how they are coming along; also check the potatoes. Season to taste with more salt and pepper and top up with extra water/stock, if necessary.

When the lentils and potatoes are cooked, remove the casserole dish from the heat and let it rest for 5 minutes with the lid on. To serve, spoon the lentils into individual bowls and drizzle with olive oil. My mum used to put a small splash of white wine vinegar in her bowl as well – something for you to experiment with. Enjoy with some lovely crusty bread.

Lentejas al Argelino

Warm, spicy Puy lentils with harissa, caramelised red onions, tomatoes and lemon juice

Hamdi, our head chef, makes a delicious, spicy lentil dish that would make my mum proud. He uses Puy lentils (or the Spanish equivalent, Padina lentils) because they keep their texture when they're cooked. You can use other lentils, if you wish, but pay attention to the cooking time on the packet.

Serves 4

500g **Puy lentils** (or lentils of your choice)
1/2 teaspoon **harissa paste** (see page 11)
olive oil
2 **tomatoes** (seeds removed), finely chopped
1 large **red onion**, finely chopped
juice of 1/2 **lemon**
Maldon sea salt and **cracked black pepper**, to taste

Check the lentils for any stones, then place them in a large pan of salted water, bring to the boil and simmer for 40 minutes. When done, drain and tip into a large bowl. Put the harissa in a cup and add 6 dashes of olive oil, stirring it in well. Spoon the dressing over the lentils, add the finely chopped tomatoes and mix everything together really well.

Pour 6 dashes of olive oil into a frying pan, add the chopped onions and fry on a low heat, stirring regularly, until soft. Remove with a slotted spoon and leave to cool, and then stir into the lentils, along with the lemon juice. Season to taste with salt and pepper, and then leave to stand for 1 hour (or preferably until the next day) to develop the flavours.

Preheat your oven to 150°C/300°F/gas mark 2. Just before you are ready to serve, spoon the lentils into individual ovenproof bowls and place in the middle of the oven to warm through for 5 minutes, or longer if needed. Give the lentils a final stir and drizzle over a little olive oil.

puddings

Over the years we have had our fair share of talented people in the kitchen. All of them have cooked up a 'savoury' storm, but none of them have excelled in the pudding department. On my thirty-fifth birthday, one of our original chefs very kindly made me a chocolate cake. I think in its parallel universe at the time it had been a door stop, because, quite frankly, it was inedible! Over the years new chefs came, and we tried making different puds, but none showed any promise – and so we stuck to our repertoire of five puddings.

Customers often enquire about different ones, my cousin Francis being one of them – with a cheek, she always insists on seeing the menu knowing full well there is nothing new – but we know they like what we do serve and we make them consistently well. Three of the puds are house-made – the chocolate mousse, the flan and the rice pudding. Our most recent addition is the cheesecake, which is made by Patrick's nephew's wife, Ania. The only pudding that isn't homemade is the almond tart, which we buy in from one of our Spanish suppliers (C&D Wines), and the ice-creams, which come from Marine Ices in Camden.

We had one particular chef who I would find having a slice of cake with his morning coffee (I share his opinion that it is the best way to enjoy the cake... with a good cup of milky coffee) to which he would always say, 'quality control' whilst scoffing his face.

Bollo de Limón

Auntie Annie's lemon cake

My Aunt Anita would always make us this lovely lemon cake whenever she came to visit, and she still does to this day. It is light and fresh, but not too sweet. My aunt always makes it in a 20cm cake tin with a cavity in the middle so it looks like a Polo mint (a ring mould), but you can use a normal one if you prefer.

Serves 8

275g **self-raising flour**
110g **caster sugar**
grated rind and juice of 1 **lemon**
2 **eggs**
150ml **olive oil**
1 x 125g carton **lemon yogurt**
1 x 20cm round cake tin, buttered

Preheat your oven to 180°C/350°F/gas mark 4.

In a large mixing bowl, combine the flour, sugar and lemon rind. Make a well in the centre and add the eggs, olive oil, yogurt and lemon juice. Stir everything together carefully to form a smooth mixture, and then pour into the prepared cake tin. Bake in the oven for 45 minutes, or until the cake is risen and golden and a sharp knife inserted into the centre comes out clean. Leave to stand in the tin for a few minutes, and then turn out onto a wire rack to cool completely. Serve with cream or ice-cream.

Bizcocho de Almendras y Pasas

Mum and dad's almond and sultana cake

And then my Mum and Dad came along with their own take on the Lemon Cake. Back when we first opened, my parents used to make us an almond and sultana cake, which was hugely popular, but when age and ill health got the better of them their little cottage industry had to close down (which is why we now buy in our almond cake from a Spanish supplier).

It was quite amusing watching my mum and dad stroll into the busy restaurant carrying a plastic shopping bag with three cakes wrapped in tin foil inside. They would walk up to the bar, take the cakes out of the bag and plonk them down. Customers would look on inquisitively as we transferred the cakes to the kitchen and ushered my parents to the their table. And those who had been waiting for their pudding to arrive, would always look up and smile at them before tucking in. My dad would always reply with 'que aproveche' – 'hope you enjoy it' – and they certainly did.

Serves 8 (2 generous slices each)

150ml **olive oil**

1 heaped tablespoon **blanched almond flakes**

275g **self-raising flour**

110g **caster sugar**

grated rind of 1 **lemon**, plus 1 tablespoon **lemon juice**

2 **eggs**

1 x 125g carton **natural yogurt**

1 heaped tablespoon **sultanas**, soaked overnight in 200ml warm water

20 **whole blanched almonds**

1 x 20cm round cake tin, buttered

Preheat your oven to 180°C/350°F/gas mark 4. Pour 30ml of the olive oil into a small frying pan and place on a low heat. Put in the almond flakes and fry gently until golden brown, paying close attention to them to ensure they don't burn. When they're done, remove them from the pan with a slotted spoon and leave to cool. Reserve the oil for later. When the almonds are cold, crush them using a pestle and mortar and leave to one side.

In a large mixing bowl, combine the flour, sugar and lemon rind. Make a well in the centre and add the eggs, the rest of the olive oil (plus the oil from the pan), the yogurt, lemon juice, sultanas and crushed almond flakes. Stir everything together to form a smooth mixture, and then pour into the prepared cake tin. Bake in the oven for 45 minutes. About 5 minutes before the cake is done, arrange the whole almonds around the top, pushing them in well, and return the cake to the oven. The cake is cooked when it is risen and golden brown on top and a sharp knife inserted into the centre comes out clean. Leave to stand in the tin for a few minutes, then turn out onto a wire rack to cool completely. Serve with cream, custard or ice-cream. Or drizzle with Pedro Jimenez PX 1979 Gran Reserva dessert wine and serve with vanilla ice-cream.

Flan de Naranja

Orange caramel custard

'Flan', a caramel… egg custard. A classic, Spanish pudding. Now to me, it varies from the French counterpart by having higher egg content. I like that. I do not like eating cold scrambled egg, but I do like an 'egg' flavour to my flans. Call me a heathen… but that is how I came to know them from a very young age. My mum and aunts all cooked their flans in a similar fashion and when the recipe was introduced at El Parador, we stuck to it. The basic recipe can be used to make flans of different flavours by substituting another liquid for part, or all of the milk. A few years ago, we changed the recipe and added some orange zest to the caramel, which subtly infused the egg mixture rather than changed it completely. This change did not go down well with some of our regulars, namely our mate Nick Buzzard. He bends our ears back every time. But we have the support and backing of the rest of his 'darts team' Ed and Kathy. Sorry Nick!

Serves 12 … roughly

for the caramel
200g **sugar**
1/2 **orange zest**

for the egg custard
3 **eggs**
100ml **single cream**
1/2 tablespoon **sugar**
600ml **whole milk**

Preheat your oven to 170°C/325°F/gas mark 3.

Prepare the caramel first. Put the sugar in a deep saucepan and pour in enough water to cover it. Boil until the sugar melts and caramelises. Two warnings: don't let it burn and be very careful as it is extremely hot.

When the sugar has all caramelised, take it off the heat and stir in the orange zest and then pour into a clear, heatproof dish, about 13cm by 22cm. Spread it around so it covers the bottom. You can use individual moulds, but it is much easier to use one and serve it from there. Let it cool down and leave to one side.

Whisk thoroughly the eggs, cream, milk and sugar and pour into the mould. Sit the mould in a large ovenproof dish. Carefully pour in enough boiling water to come about 2.5cm up the side of the large dish (this is called a bain marie). Put on the middle shelf of the oven and bake for 50 minutes to 1 hour. From time to time, check to see if it has set. The surface will have browned and become firm to touch. Insert a knife into it to double check its firmness. Leave to cool, then refrigerate overnight. Serve the next day with double cream… ice-cream… lovely rich Pedro Ximenez Reserva 1979 dessert wine – yummy!

Marquesa de Chocolate

Chocolate mousse with orange liqueur

A must for chocolate fiends. Always use good-quality chocolate, and stick to the alcohol measures: too much just overpowers everything.

Serves 4

4 **egg whites**

1 tablespoon **caster sugar**

300ml **whipping cream**

300g good-quality dark or milk **chocolate**

50ml **orange liqueur** of your choice

Place the egg whites in a mixer and whisk until stiff. Add the caster sugar and keep whisking until stiff and shiny. Spoon into a large bowl.

Clean out the mixer, pour in the whipping cream and whisk until thick.

Rest a large stainless steel bowl over a large pan of simmering water. Break up the chocolate and put it in the bowl. Allow it to melt completely, stirring from time to time, and then add the liqueur and mix well. Spoon the chocolate mixture into the mixer with the cream and whisk together. Add the egg whites and whisk again. Spoon into individual bowls (or one large one) and refrigerate overnight before serving.

Arroz con Leche del Parador

El Parador rice pudding

Rice pudding: dry or wet; with or without skin; hot or cold; baked or cooked in a saucepan; cinnamon or nutmeg; loved or hated… the debate continues. My mum used to bake it, slightly dry, no skin and used both cinnamon and nutmeg. She crossed boundaries so to speak. It was great hot and cold. El Parador's version is cooked in a saucepan. It is moist with a hint of sweetness and cinnamon and can be eaten hot or cold.

Serves 6

240g **pudding rice**

1 1/4 litre **milk**

100g **sugar**

1/2 tablespoon **ground cinnamon**

Put the milk in a saucepan and bring to the boil. Add the rice, sugar and cinnamon and simmer, uncovered, until the rice is tender. Serve straight away with a dusting of cinnamon or nutmeg or you can dollop in a spoonful of some lovely fruit compote. If you want a skin, just put the bowls under the grill to brown the tops of the puddings.

Like porridge, you can add almost any fresh fruit in the last few minutes of cooking and it will infuse the dessert. You can also add 50ml of single cream to make it extra creamy.

Pastel de Queso

Mixed berry swirl cheesecake

Patrick's nephew Rowan came in one day extolling the virtues of his wife's cheesecake, which beggared the retort: 'the proof of the pudding is in the eating'. That we did and it proved to be deliciously creamy and light. Ania changes the flavours regularly.

Serves 12

for the fruit filling
300g frozen **mixed berries** (such as blueberries, raspberries and/or blackberries), defrosted or fresh if in season
60g **caster sugar**

for the base
190g **shortbread biscuits**
100g **almond meal**
70g melted **butter**

for the filling
175g **caster sugar**
900g **full-fat cream cheese**
250g **crème fraîche**
3 **eggs**

1 x 26cm Springform cake tin

Place the fruit and caster sugar in a deep, heavy-based pan. Set over a medium heat and stir until the sugar has dissolved. Bring to the boil, and then simmer for 5 minutes, or until thick. Spoon into a large mixing bowl and leave to cool for a minimum of 90 minutes.

Preheat your oven to 130°C/275°F/gas mark 1.

For the base, crush the biscuits in a food-processor. Add the almond meal and melted butter, and then blitz again. Spoon the mixture into your cake tin and press down well, making the edges slightly taller. Chill in the fridge until set.

For the filling, put in the cream cheese in the food-processor and blitz until smooth. Add the crème fraîche, eggs and sugar and blitz again.

Spoon 90 per cent of the cream cheese filling into the cooled fruit mixture and fold in thoroughly until a solid colour has formed. Pour over the base.

Drizzle over the remaining cream cheese filling and swirl it around with a knife to create a marbled pattern on top.

Place the cheesecake in the oven and cook for 60–70 minutes, or until set. When it is done, take it out of the oven and run a thin knife around the outer edge to release the pressure and prevent the surface from cracking as it cools. Leave to cool in the tin, and then refrigerate and serve cold.

George Orwell once said, 'man only stays human by preserving large patches of simplicity in his life'. We try and cook food as simply as possible. The more ingredients you add to any dish, the more complicated it becomes, and consequently, more difficult to execute. You have to think about flavours and balance. The more balls a juggler tosses around the more difficult it becomes for him to keep an eye on things. You can try... cooking is about trying and tasting. El Parador is not a 'cutting edge' restaurant, pushing the boundaries of culinary endeavours. We are a local neighbourhood restaurant, serving good, unpretentious, honest food. It is thanks to our chefs Hamdi, Cob, Jack and August and the quality of their cooking that makes our job in the front a lot easier.

Before we first opened, a friend of ours in the industry told us that along the way all sorts of people would come and tell us how to do things. He told us to stay focused and do what we thought was best. To date, that has been the soundest piece of advice we have received, because so far, it has worked. In our second year, we asked a customer what he thought of our food. He said: 'sack the chef'. We did not, and that particular customer became a regular, often complimenting the same chef he advised to be sacked.

Family and friends have all helped forge El Parador and helped us put across our ethos of simplicity and quality. My wife Sarah and our two grown-up children, Charlotte and Ben, help out on front of house as do Patrick's nephew Rowan and Edward, Juliet's son. Rowan worked with Ania, who eventually became his wife and they now have two children. Cob's son Mathew also lends a hand every so often. That warmth and personal approach has helped our customers feel 'at home', relaxed and welcome.

We have had our fair share of celebrities come in. No-one gets bothered... they eat in peace. We have another customer, Bob Lamm, who comes to eat with us as soon as he gets off the plane from NYC. As well as being a regular customer, he has become a good friend. We often swap stories and news via email. We have made many good friends who, like Bob, originally came in as customers. Some of them have become close friends (here's looking at you Adrian Chipperfield) who have given us massive support and encouragement over the years. Some have unfortunately passed away but will always be with us. Over the years we have welcomed some in as young children (Peter and Linda Jones and their lovely children, Alex, Laura and Nick), watched them grow, and then, as time marches on, have welcomed them in as young adults... bringing their mates in with them... and so the cycle continues.

All this is what El Parador is about... this and the food.

top: Carlos's family enjoying a typically Spanish lunch; bottom left: Carlos feeding his pet chicken; bottom right: Carlos in the cowboy hat with his uncle (centre), aunt (right) and parents (top left and centre); on page 172: Patrick and Carlos

index

Our thanks go to our families, chefs, staff, customers and suppliers for helping us to make El Parador what it is today... a good, local neighbourhood restaurant. We would also like to thank Sophie Allen and all the team at Kyle Cathie for having patience with us... and faith.

books we love:

Rick Stein's Seafood – fantastic knowledge, instruction and clear explanations. All you need to know about seafood is in this book.
North Atlantic Seafood – an incredible encylopaedia. A fantastic read as well!
The Moro Cookbook – the first one, beautiful recipes that work.

list of suppliers:

Food:
- Products From Spain (Robert, George, Beatrice and Mirabelle) 020 8965 7274
- Kirbys Vegetable Produce (Darryl and Nicky) 020 7622 494
- Wicker Fisheries (John Exley and Tommy Wicker) 020 8986 9213
- Frank Godfrey Butchers (Peter, Philip and Jeremy) 020 7561 1713
- 1 Catch Seafoods (Sol) 020 8808 8970
- Casa Conde (Noelia) 020 7639 2800
- Woods Dry Goods (Darren) 020 8997 2211
- Exeter Street Bakery 020 7845 6462
- Marine Ices 020 7482 9000

Wine & Beers:
- Moreno Wines (Marcel, Abi, Manuel, Carlos and Inga) 020 8960 7161
  La Copa Tempranillo, Mirador Rioja, Navajas Tinto Crianza, Guelbenzu Azul Crianza, Tio Nio Crianza, PX Pedro Jimenez Gr.Reserva Dessert Wine, Santiago Sauvignon Blanc, Marques de Alella, Txacoli, De Fefinanes, Mirador Rioja Rose, Valdespino Sherries
- Alliance Wines (Alexis & Nuria) 01505 506065
  Santa Rosa Sangioviese, Quinta de Ventozelo 03, Quinta de Ventozelo 10 yr Tawny, Quinta de Ventozelo Vintage '00 Port, Buil y Gine Priorat, Nosotros Pinot Noir, Finca La Sierpe, One Chain Chardonnay, Mantel Blanco Verdejo, Luis Canas Crianza, Laus Gewurztraminer
- C+D Wines and Foods (Andres & Marga) 020 8778 1711
  Guitian Godelo, Mahou Cinco Estrellas
- Caves de Pyrennes (Gideon) 01483 554 755
  Cerro Punta Negra Shiraz, Casa Azul Merlot, Viu Manet Malbec, Winery of Good Hope Chenin Blanc
- Antoine Peterson (Antoine) 0845 658 0370
  Vera de Estenas Crianza, Mas Deu Crianza, Casa Don Angel Malbec (Spain), Castillo de Sajasarra Res. Blanco Flor, Vina Carmina Rose,
- Waterloo Wines 020 7403 7967
  L'Hereu Raventos I Blanc Cava, El Preludi
- Astrum Wines (Mark Aperna) 020 8870 5252
  Russolo Refosco Riserva (Italy), Pecorino (White wine), Italy

Catering Equipment:
- Nelsons Catering (Andy Bugge) 020 8993 9168

Flowers
- Dorotea Daniel 07792892877